PAUL BLACKBURN

THE JOURNALS

Edited By

ROBERT KELLY

BLACK SPARROW PRESS • LOS ANGELES • 1975

Some of these poems have appeared, in this or earlier form, in the following periodicals: *Almanac: 17 Poets; Anonym; Boss; Caterpillar* (and *A Caterpillar Anthology*); *Friendly Local Press; Intrepid; Lampeter Muse; Lillabullero; Mulch; Noose; Odda Tala; Promethean; Sumac; Transition; The World.*

Walter Hamady's Perishable Press published two chapbooks in extremely limited editions: *Gin* (comprising "Birds/Amsterdam," "Train to Amersfoort," "Wet," and "Gin") and *The Blue Mounds Entries.*

Library of Congress Cataloging in Publication Data

Blackburn, Paul.
    The journals.

    I. Title.
PS3552.L342J68   1975   811'.5'4   75-25714
ISBN 0-87685-240-1
ISBN 0-87685-239-8 pbk.

THE JOURNALS to my mind are Blackburn's quintessential work, and demonstrate the way his work knew to go, the power of music he could charm out of everything that came his way, or even looked as if it were thinking about it. The poems and entries are also his last work. The latest writing in it comes up to six weeks of his death in September 1971. From his papers, it is clear that in those last weeks he tried to collect the Journal pages together, and did sense them (as many of his readers from 1968 onward did) as a continuous and coherent book. The present text follows generally the order of what he had collected together and erratically paginated as *The Journals*. When repetitions, revisions, and versions have been taken away, our inheritance in this particular amounts to a typescript of some 160 pages.

Power. The tip he took from Pound was not a tune, but a way of finding. Of the poets working in these past three decades, I would say Blackburn is the paradigm of the processual—the one who most allowed his life and work to intertwine, who sought and found in the happenstance of experience a mysterious beauty called music when we hear it, that is, the Form made clear. His work reads the wayside signs and covert signatures, and is alert to every coincidence, analogy, trick of the light.

To say these things amounts to saying that Blackburn was a formal poet—he sought form and found form. He worked hard enough at the trobadors and their prosodies to qualify, had he chosen, as a walking book of meters and 'forms'—but those collected shapes were not the forms that concerned him. What form can be *discovered* as one moves through life? So his forms are always innovative, sometimes mimetic (because he loved descriptions and people and simple alignments and catalogues), but more often directly expressive of the interaction of the thing seen with the man seeing.

And very much he loved to see. Early in 1971 it became apparent to Paul and his friends that something was very wrong with his body. By mid-March, that something had been called cancer, with all the death-knell sounded. But it seems to me, without sentimental hindsight, that a few years before, certainly as early as spring 1968, Paul had intimations of death upon him. From that point forth his work, especially *The Journals*, reads like a *carni vale*, a joyous farewell to the flesh of the world. Spain, Italy, Occitan, the places he had loved and worked in on and off for twenty years, now saw him again for the last time. And the new places, California and the western mountains, he began to rack up among his knowns.

Blackburn died young, as these things are reckoned in longaeval America, but his farewell was leisurely, intensely scrutinizing the whole show again. Autumn and harvest, drive the last sweetness into the grape—all the images Europe has given us, from Ausonius to

Rilke, of what it means to live on earth and then, suddenly or with warning, not to live there any more. These things talk in Blackburn's last work, strange melancholy unusual in our people, who know how to want with urgency or reject with bitterness, but hardly ever this old world song, relishing, departing, going.

Paradox, not of Blackburn but of America, that the voice that is most our own is truest to the older sequence. Very strange. In New York, which was most his home and center, he could find the sunlight on a wall not different from Barcelona. We can warm ourselves there.

What I most value in *The Journals* is the further transcendence of the closed poem (that museum piece, that haunting but snake-filled urn) his work had long been moving from. And what gave his achievement of the open poem its peculiar power is, in some awful and simple way, just how well he could sing. He is among those to whom we must turn if we would learn how music is not dependent on its earlier conditions or social contexts. So many who have tried to open form (whatever that may mean truly) have cast away (if ever they had it) the sonorous particularity of their own breath, their integral, their own. After the mid-1950s, there is a developing pattern whereby Paul's idiolect in the written language comes closer and closer to his idiolect in the spoken language; far from making the poems bland or conversational, the syntax grows deeper roots, twists, recovers, holds attention as no singsong could. Learning so to be honest in ear and mouth, he spoke his mind. As a result, the falsity of pastoral could not finally attract him, much as he loved olive and goat and maiden. More to his point and his time, he can sing straight (a phrase he used time and again earlier on) from the city and about the city, accepting it as the natural condition of man in a way few other poets have understood. Between the earlier generation of experimenters who imagined taxi dissonance and tohu-bohu represented the city, and the latter-day meta-hicks who turn away, Paul is one of the very few American poets who have been able to address their work sanely and coherently in the midst of the ordinary condition of contemporary man. A man, he is himself everywhere, and everything becomes natural to him. As Pound showed us long ago, the natural is the most difficult to come to, to say.

To the music nothing is trivial. To the composer of these poems, no idle dailiness was without its seed of connection. A New York poet, as they say, happiest in the middle of things, a stranger to scorn. It was all around him, and he could handle it. From what seem the most casual notations of place and event, Blackburn's formal intelligence discovers a new order rooted in content and inextricable from it, even if the deft musician willed it away.

RK

Table of Contents

THE JOURNALS

How is it I keep remembering
after all those / these facts,
                    this flack
        keeps . coming?
It all drives back upon the brain .
After yesterday, two things were
plain-ly set against the mindfall
        The sandspit in Arkansas
        after a motorcycle ride in the November day
            was warmed   3 cigarettes & talk
Or how explain the marks of branches in the
sand, with no mantrack near . Complexities
            of the very simple—what?
                Standing at the
                edge of   I had to pee
                into the Mississippi . And
later, cottonheaded from whiskey,
did not spend, tho she did from my
tongue . this young wife
of someone else, too up tight from
cars & bikes pulling into the driveway
where was her car? It had run
                out of gas . o yes.
The anxiety (plus too much whiskey) kept me down .
Here was a quim I wanted to do wonderful things in
taste was sweet and sour
The rest had left : Bobby & Lee on bike
it must have been damnably cold
that hour of morning
Bobby's nose falling off . the wind
up Lee's sleeves . And all for
a spider hanging inconclusively
swinging, flowers in the vermouth
bottle, yellow, chrysanthemums, cost 75 ¢ a bunch
            at the market as opposed .

Two cups of coffee and the magazine in
the bathroom . would be .

CYCLE WORLD 1966 . The Road Test
Annual . which only Sara
wins . An-other
terrible Sunday morning in the world,
everybody juiced and coffeed
Memphis is on the river, cold
Sunday paper on the porch &   torch
the flowers stand
        there
the motor warming up
            turning over
The arm stretches out again
to
    no / one /there .

UNCHARTED

SUN is that
rare in Paris,   I
          almost swim in it

The day accomplishes itself with its
          small failures & annoyances

Its pleasures mount gently toward evening
walking many strange streets toward

home, it were, no map, O Joan!
Let me come before you a triumph and
          a happy man!

THE EXPENSIVE MEAL

Par la main
jusqu'à la source

       By hand, he sed
    to the headwaters of it all, where

       everyone begins, be-
   gins, whiskeys, cognacs, le bien, c'est
de payer la différence, and the man
who runs the cloakroom & has his tips from that
    polishes the glasses
    when there's no one splitting out, it's
a way of doubling it up, I love

the SERIOUSNESS of it, how they all take it,
                  hard or well, you
give them all le pourboire, they've done well or badly.
It is not true.

I blow my nose on some toilet tissue
from the hotel, the
young man wiping glasses notices it, his
         neutral face, that
   increases his tip   .   BLOW
everyone's mind, the

    only way to do it .

Green shoes
black umbrella
stands on her good legs outside the school for an hour.
Checks her watch & vistas of
doorways, corners . People pass

      Alas, neither she nor he.
He's in Memphis and lord only knows where she is . The
rainfall, the umbrella, the watch, the green shoes,
the green rainbow, the umbra, watch the shoes, they
move, see?

      □

Kiss / kiss!   A
& I do   miss   B L U E S
you .
Let me be where
that next
other glorious morning
      will be
& not in the mind either, babe,
not never no more in the mind
babe, not never no more in the mind .

      □

Cold birds out the window trying to sing
Sweep of the sea . moving water . much further away
      I got rights
      to be blue, noo?
Who are we?
Let us see
    a gull   and a porpoise
¿cómo no?
      better
than any marriage I have had or
      could think of .

      □

"I've been fixin a hole where the rain comes in"
& below is 17th Street, Nashville, the
cross-thru below Fisk campus
                                    where is
LIQUOR STOREs, BARs, CLEANERS, numerous BARBER SHOPs,
burger joints, a movie, & even a gas station, ES-
SO es . y no es . si-saw . So.
Off they go, back to Memphis,
                    tank full of gas and a
                    pocketful of rye .
The rest of this town is located else-where
        DOWN-TOWN . and is scary as shit
mean white mouths and steel eyes out
gunning for my beard and long hair and tight jeans
The eyes say it loud and hard   NIGGUHLOVUH!   and
I surely am, all the beautiful faces I see downtown
are black . a pleasure to take bus back
                    to the ghetto, that's where it is, Morton .
            I am a nun here for days
                            soon shortened.

Where were all they
        &
it was not me . When it was
I was there.

"How is you spell PO-EMS, man?

                        □

If you're looking
        for where it is where
        it really is, never
        choose no road . What
        ever road you take will
        tell you, make you go
                take you
                        to
where
it
is
REALLY.

BIRDS / AMSTERDAM

Flurry of fat sparrows hits the fence
top near the Oude Turfmarkt, whence

        look very surprised
        to have made it
        look around

      10 notes   2 chords
      I try to sightread
      the melody / too fast, they've gone

In the tiny square NW side of the
Leidseplein   where is a carpark   the
trees are full of grackles   .   Taxi
stand   .   taxidriver, no fare, stops
briefly, gets out, slams his door,
walks to the nearest (one of the youngest) trees
& kicks it
               hard & high   .   the sky
is blackened   .   the ears attacked

      The driver smiles
      The big birds circle
      drift & land again
He gets back in the car and drives off.
Still smiling

At the Dam by Moses Aaronstraat
the Sunday afternoon is filled with
solid citizens, their overcoated arms, shoulders
loaded with pigeons doing the neck-ring peck
:   little girls with their hands full
The pigeons cluster & waddle & fly
in packs, circle up to the roofs & back
& keep the air full of wings   .   to be fed

Prinsengracht   .   Herengracht   .   Singelgracht
    families   .   flocks / quack
      it's ducks swimming along leaving
      delicate wakes along the quiet canals
      Well, not so quiet   .   QUACK

Sarphatipark   /   Vondelpark
a few songbirds   (more grackles,
more sparrows) . Amsterdamsebos
more of the same plus some few
swans, mean-beaked, very white, plus

                              EVERYWHERE
                                 my gulls

                         above rooftops, on them,
                         into backyards, over canals
              bridges, parks & markets,
              business streets, Centraal Station,
              the Amstel, the Singel, Rokin,
              Osdorp & Slotermeer, Entrepôtdok,
              Het ij, Dijksgracht, Ertshaven

Mostly the birdsound
in this town is harsh
&   in/over everywhere
my gulls
hustle food

                         big & tough or
                         small & compact
                         they make it

              tho the Paleis on the Dam
              belongs to the pigeons

But, I'd heard all that about storks
nesting in chimneys   .   did not see any storks
Where are the storks?

                              Nov. 18-20, 1967
                              Amsterdam

TRAIN TO AMERSFOORT

Sheep staring
dully across a field

          three white pigs in another

in a third,   7   black & white cows
grazing along, their heads down, tails lifted .

Line of trees far off.

Sheep
more sheep
more cows
more pigs, cluster of
distant cows, two horses
heads lifted this time, tails lifted also .
Whole herds of seagulls walk in the fields
sheepdung . cowturds . pigshit .
Small
      canals
run thru the cold November day's
           green foggy morning
near an arm of the North Sea near
               Naarden Bussum

before the railroad turns from the sea
toward Hilversum .

WET

Goats trot and feed among the oil refineries
Cows lie down in the fields . short pieces of rope
tied to one horn to lead them in .
Small feeder canals, the flat landscape
broken by trees . an insistent green . den Haag to Rotterdam

      Two horses, one feeding, the
      other scratches his rump on the high
      power
      transmission tower . The shaggy goats .

GIN

Clear objects, the
clear objections   .   The gulls
float thru the yard   .   The wall-
paper is stained, sections are
pure Cretan linear-B .

        I fled New York somehow,
        it's all her's now . And cold .

Amsterdam is full of sun, it falls
aslant ten buildings in the next street
I can see from my window—the Dutch
      believe in large windows, it
is exactly the width of the room, a long narrow
Van Gogh-room, even the skinny bed
      in the right position .
Except the canal is at the front of the ho-tel,
so the room faces
what I wd / call
the wrong direction.

        Black roofs and red roofs   .   Tile.
        While,
blackbirds in the shadowed backyard
hop about thru bright yellow leaves, or
flap between the lower branches .

An enormous gull just swooped thru the yards
      leisure-ly .

The canal at the front of the ho-tel,
go to it   .   Read the cards.

        Even with sunlight, I am lightly depressed .
        Foto, September 18, the boat-train
        Le Havre to Paris   .   Joan confronts
        the French landscape   .   the gold locket,
her toothmarks in it . Good, tight

lens on that camera.   Blue
dress, blue landscape blurred

       O shit,
       I left my heart in the 7th arrondissement
       a good bit South of here, apparently.

       Forget it. I've left my heart everywhere,
       walk around collecting bits and shards .

Gil, how do you keep
such a unified vision of your own
       lives / & parts?

I take trains / or planes

       boats / or goats

Gull flies thru the backyard one way
crosses pigeon flying thru the other   .   Damn,

this gin is good!

RUE DES LOIS

Le miracle, ça, c'est arrivé enfin .
Ici, après un sombre hiver, c'est voir
          cet homme
     qui regarde sa ville,
qui se promène dans l'air
          sur sa terre,
le soleil toujours pâle sur les murs,
mais dans l'air du printemps
contemplant le soleil sur les murs
     flairant, la tête haute,
pas un regard pour la vitrine d'une librairie
qui a pris
cinq minutes de son attention
chaque fois qu'il était passé
          tout l'hiver .

PARIS-TOULOUSE TRAIN

Caersi (Quercy)

Roads
run off into the countryside & lanes
    into the trees & disappear . The hills .

At Brive, the first thing I see
is a young wife standing in her dooryard, a
chick, in red coat, black slacks, a yellow sweater, not
    taking any chances . the Corrèze:

that river kept coming at us from the left
side of the train, at an angle .
    At Gourdon, shades of de Born,
I hear the rhythms of the old speech. Two gents
in the next booth in the dining car speaking a
Language thought to be dead the last 700 years—
they talk abt the lack of feeling in politics these days .
    shades of Guillem .

Okay, I'm home but not safe yet, whole
    stretches of rapids . Can
you think of any better entry to the south, what
    anyway, goes on in yr mind? Tree
that it will be,
hill, that it will,
field that it see, mist that it
was Joan's mouth I kissed
before I left Paris, fog
that I dig . December, be kind
to me .

Cahors

Tileyard, lumberyard, a
medieval bridge, towers
at both ends, & in the middle .
The hill like a sleeping animal .

dormant . the
gas stations like anyplace else .

Signals 4.

POUR L'OBTENIR DE L'EAU
APPUYER SUR LA PÉDALE, it sez
& the *eau non potable*
has been carefully edited down to
          'no   pot'

And having had my taperecorder on for
four hours, the
new conductor at Montauban & his small moustache, tells me
          ''La musique—c'est interdit sur le train.''
''Forbidden to play music on the train . . .''
I figure he's got nothing else to say .

          There are
          sonsofbitches
          everywhere .

     Bonjour, monsieur Blackburn!
     Welcome back to Toulouse!
      and rain, I swear .

KARTHA
ginian lamps, shaped
like shells to fit the hand –2 flames–
one lifting at each end of that beautiful curve, did they
            join?   Lovers' lamps .
               put in some oil & see

& Etruscan cups, five/six
centuries before that god came down, all
         jet-black
         with big ears
         held like a dipper,
         probably dipped in the jar –
         spill
a bit onto the floor first, for the gods

The guards
who'd confiscated my camera stayed
down by the *caisse* at the entrance
so I touched all the statues of Venus
cunt, belly and breasts
all those of Bacchus & Hercules
I tickled under the balls, just to be sure .

& Lucius Verus (161-169 A.D.)
looked just like Robert David . I passed
a pleasant hour with the goddess, the gods .

PLAZA REAL WITH PALM TREES : second take

B A R C E L O N A ! This city again
after   10   years of separation, exile
maybe a better term   .   is warm
and busy

Early in January, I've just seen my friends to the train back
to France   .   poor friends   .   And my Joan, weeping briefly in
the compartment   .   a good girl—will
                        be a good woman soon—all there .
It's been a beautiful   18 days—half of it here on the Ramblas,
sun from late morning to late afternoon, then Valencia, Cullera,
Faro, Alicante, train & bus, then, on impulse, the boat to Palma

                    ''bound upon a magic ship
                       for a land I'd never see''
                           well, not quite .

Seen the first time in   10   years, was very good, even if
for two days only.   And walking back from the Estación de Francia
here, the train had pulled out sometime during that walk—I cldnt
stay to cry myself—

                    but dove back
                    into the city .   This city!

The slow walk back to the pension, a manzanilla at the Bodega Reus,
small streets, no cars, people walk in the streets .

DIUMENGA   /   SUNDAY

Here, people carry their children
no pushcarts or baby carriages, they
carry them
in their arms .
                    Both arms if they are mothers,
                    perhaps a single arm if they are
FATHERS—that simple,
complicated act of becoming
that kind of man, finally, but the kids—
one arm or two, RIDE there at ease
Looking about them, digging the scene

27

—big eyes for my beard and long hair wd/ be bigger had I
worn the cowboy hat, or the Mexican, they

eat their pasteles or sweets
& stare

            The mothers worry that I am
            looking at their legs (of
            course, that's what I'm doing) the men
            worry or don't—it's Sunday .

Calle de Avino, I'm
behind a young man and his girl:
all of us walking toward the Ramblas
Just below Caracoles, a drunken American beachcomber-type lunges
toward them, reaches for the girl.
The little guy coldcocks him with one stiff arm, doesn't even
break his step . The big blond American staggers from the resistance,
turns and yells
          "Hey, YOU!"

    The young cat turns, I'm passing
    the drunk, I say,
    mean & quiet : "Lay off 'em."
    but loud enuf everyone could hear.

The young Catalan looks at me,
I make the Ballantine sign with my fingers & grin   .   I'm back
in Barcelona

wander up toward the Plaza Real & the pension, have
a short discussion about travel & sexual mores with
the aging faggot on the desk & come upstairs to look out the window.

I live in a tree these days
The pigeons are trotting about
Around noon (still Sunday), a few hours ago, the
square was filled with stamp collectors
with their books,
of stamps, buying & selling
         trading
         in sunlight,
         under palmtrees waving .
Now, at   4,   young Spanish hipsters stand
their hips against the fountain's railing
         or in clumps

                        the winter sunlight fading .

Girls in skirts impossible 10 years ago
                —that short now—arrive, leave—
                with or without young men
It's Spain still & chances are they stall, they
leave with the girlfriend they arrived with
Tho maybe in the same direction
as the boys, tho maybe—
still, they've no place to go   .   it's money

The pigeons stroll
the people stand or move
                but TALK,
THIS TOWN!

                The old man in dark glasses
                who sells the peanuts & sweets
                has been leaning against the
                same palm tree for   6   hours now .
                his old wife relieves him a couple hours at noon .

Families pass thru
carrying the youngest ones .
Here, people carry their children
No baby carriages in this square, they
carry them in their arms, their
children dig it
                —everything .

                □

                Once again, I am *looking* at it
                (down into the street with glazed eyes)
                Sounds of voices
                drift up to the pension window
                thru it, tho it be winter, O
                sweet christ, go down, go
                down there, man,
                        into the real plaza, the
                        Plaza Real itself, either
enter your life, enter its life,

or make yr/own

□

By   10   at nite the young studs
've gathered in groups of 7 or   12,
with one girl, perhaps, to each group
to keep the game going

           Groups of 4 with no girl, just
           talk—go down, go
           down, enter the dance
                       (evening, Kelly)
Joan, Dean & Sandy
are back in France by now, pobrecitos.
  France, this winter, not only de Gaulle
   & inflation, but notably
     snow, floods, rain .
     Hugo wrote *Les Misérables*, he
               wasn't kidding, those
               people are poor in their hearts, O
fuck France, fuck its rain, fuck its
mail chutes, I ought

never go back again . It's
still Sunday .

□

Wipe it out for an hour .
Go eat .

           The boys now highly reduced
           to 5 and 9 .
           Two American chicks at a table
           of the café nearest calle Fernando
                 "... highly unnecessary—"
no words I can use. The *Glorita*, alone,
this time . sopa . canelones . ternura .
My *Ideales con papel trigo*, the old-fashioned
black cigarettes with wheat paper, found unexpectedly
on the Born in Palma
are such a rarity here, the waiter asks me one .
I say, "10 years ago . . ."
he sez "10 years ago."

A professional American couple, but quiet, the
next table down, he probably teaches:
"Paul will know," he sez confidently, not loud .
I hope he's right.   The waiter & I
both enjoy our cigarettes .
The waiter's so happy, matter of fact, he
forgets that I ordered *flan* & brings
an orange—
The *naranja*'s name is   TIPICA   & iss
tamped on its side / is
a navel orange & seedless . O, the gods!

What we need here, soldier, is more carts, more navels,
carts & horses, more burros, & less cavilling,
take the lead out of it!   I make room to spit out seeds
that do not exist, just habit .

Joan is asleep on the Paris train,
it is passing Toulouse about now .
She doesn't wake up . Nods .

Back in the street
Fernando is all lit up, so's
calle de la Unión to the other side,
& the Ramblas .
It looks like Christmas.   Baby,
it ain't .

January 8, 1968
Barcelona .

31

R O A D S

Having been on
the road

      ALL   THIS   TIME

(three months plus & it's not stopped anywhere yet)
               run baby, run, you
               won't get anywhere until
               you
               stop
(somewhere)
and even then &
even then

Thus qualified, I
want to write a poem abt / roads
that they are there, that
one travels them & is not obtuse
nor obliged to take anymore in, onto the mind, than
the body in time and space taketh unto itself, the
mind in its holy vacuum
breaking out of   past the fact
to other   FACTS?
           give me something
          anything else to pad
        this hard straightbacked
      chair, say that bed, Joan in it .   that's
    padding, that's bedding or
  railroading .   featherbedding?

R O A D S . nowhere
I can stay for long, it goes
by itself for a long time unattended by more than
fences along it   .   what the wind constructs   .   its own
silly protection, keeping the monsters back in
that idyllic pasture we call mind   .   O, find the
nearest next intersection, the road goes on
until it meets another
road, and then rose up, it rises up, that choice

32

not so much taken
as come to
where we sit down in the middle
and let it all roll over us . Or
Lew Welch's gig: "Take a few steps off it
& the whole incredible machinery rolls by,
not seeing us at all."

                    (Or, even further out, that naval
                    lieutenant commander out on the end of a
                    line in space, now on postage stamps, said:
                    "There is absolutely no distortion and
                    I'm not coming back in.")

so there's this road
& one stays on it forever until one
(it) stops (roads
go on forever, so do parentheses) or
gets some WHERE else in his body or his head,
finds there's another place to be, comes
or goes
quietly to one side, & there
lives
or dies
accident
-ly .

Hawk turns into the sun
over the sea, wings red, the
turn upward   .   mountain behind me

I have left those intricate mountains
My face now to the simple Mediterranean   .   flat .
small boats .   gulls .   the blue

Old hawk
is still there tho, as
there are foxes on these barren mountains .
   Old man in a beret, 62 perhaps, came
   into the village bar the other day
   —2 skins and one fox unskinned—

   "You hunted those down?"

   "I hunted them. They
   come closer in winter, seeking food,
   there isn't much up there—"

Rocky headland down into the Gulf of Valencia .
My windows face North.   He was a hawk .

I turn back to the Rockies, to the
valley swinging East, Glenwood to Aspen, up
the pass, it is darkest night the hour before dawn,
Orion, old Hunter, with whom
I may never make peace again, swings
just over the horizon at 5 o'clock
as I walk   .   The mountains fade into light

Being together there was never enuf,—it was
"my thing"   Nothing of importance (the reach)
was ever said .   I turn
and say farewell to the valley, those hills .
A physical part of wellbeing's been spent or
left there—goodbye   mountains   valley,
all.   Never

34

to be there again   .   Never.

It is
an intricate dance
to turn & say goodbye
to the hills we live in the presence of .
when mind dies of its time
it is not the place goes away .

      Now, the hawk turns in the sun, circles
      over the sea .
               Defines me .
      Still the stars show thru .

Orion in winter rises early,
summer late   .   dark before .

             dawn during August
             during which day, the
             sun shines on everything.

                    Defines it .
               Shadows I do not see.

I rise early
in every season.

      The act defines me,
      even if it is not my act .

            Hawk circles over the sea .
                 My act .

Saying goodbye, finally .
Being here is not enuf, tho
I make myself part of what is real.   Recognize me
standing in that valley, taking only the embraces of friends, taking
only my farewell   .   with me
      Stone from my mountains .
      Your words are mine, at the end.

THE TISSUES

You know what has in-
vaded Europe since I
left her a dozen years ago?

T A M PAX
&
K L E E NEX

that wood to paper, cotton
grows—on the banks of the Mississippi—
that delicacy, that intimate
      (S'all cellulose)
or when are we going to send paper airplanes to Vietnam?
Disposable klenliness has come to overthrow the old world finally
Coke, Pepsi, & hamburgesas could
     never have done it alone.

'' Comment TAMPAX peut-il empêcher
   toute odeur?—Parcequ'il n'est
pas exposé à l'air, étant porté intérieurement . . .
   RIGHT! teach the ladies how to
   shove it, and what's at fault is the air!

Actually, I'm not so unhappy about the Kleenex, my
sinuses that dependent on it these years
—it's only the price I object to, usually
twice the stateside price at least—
     and having grown up
     terribly,
    in Vermont, one
thing I could never stand was a
stiff, dirty snotrag .
O handkerchiefs,
I've foregone your pleasant softness all my
life, damn near, for the flimsy softness of
papier-mouchoirs en quate de cellulose, 1,30 F, prix conseillé
75 skinny, halfsize (format moyen) for a
quarter, New York 200 fullsize for the same price .
Spain even worse, 30 ptas for the small regular 100 box
(or 45 ¢), when

for 30 ptas. I can still buy a whole meal in Barcelona
(okay, wine is extra).

The Kimberly-Clark Corporation is taking
advantage of my dripping forehead.
Fuck the Kimberly-Clark Corporation,
fuck their mailchutes.

I've just cooked up and eaten a
fryingpan full of sheeps guts
with potatoes and onions, leaving a
handful for the morning to heat my own gut with.

    A piece of wood looks like stone
    if it's worn smooth enuf by the sea—
    if it shrivels a bit, like flesh then .

I'm going to bed, turn
on the electric heater, & keep
my sinuses dry .
    Goodbye world   .   until
    morning, sea.

News of Che's death & other
political musings, Spanish
newspapers being somewhat
slow to report certain events.

Plaza de Portal de Elche
in Alicante, wet
from last night's rain .
I had the news in Paris, mid-October, sitting
in a café with Joan, picked up a leftover newspaper
from the next chair, refolded it to the frontpage.
The news is still with me .

It's eight in the morning   .   This square carries an
unintentional message in
its ancient name made new   .

        Coffee and ensaimadas at
        the kiosk set low center
        amid the gandules and palmeras
        "Grande como el grande, no ande."
¿Que quieres? this early, this late   2
taxis only on the plaza now . *"Una sombra y
dos ensaimadas,"* instead of
        "La revolución, señor, y dos ensaimadas."
¿Por favor?"

Young man stops on one corner at a
shop mirror to
squeeze a pimple or two on his way to work;
looks vacantly at the white
blood-flecked excrescence on the
thumb and middle finger of his left hand,
checks the mirror again,
              the hope of Spain .

        By 8:15 there are   4   taxis on
        the side of the square toward the port,
           2   on the lateral and   5

'minitaxis' on the side toward town .
The second coffee, this time black, with coñac,
goes down more easily .

☐

[Back at the pensión, another quality of certain Spanish
newspapers grows to be of prime importance.]

Stockingfooted down
the tiled & whitewashed
narrow hall, its full
length .

The light works, so
    sit & read :
On the something 28th,
South Yemen tossed out   30   British
    military hired a year ago when
            Yemen became independent .
Foreign Office sends a stiff note—the
Yemenites reply (politely)
that they're saving money .

And an outfit called RUTHERFORD ESPAÑOLA, S.A., at
    14, General Goded,
                in Madrid, will
build you a swimming pool shaped like your kidney
out of stone and tile   .   The
rectangles of paper are neatly
torn   .   I tear mine once more
    lengthwise, while thinking
of all the smug accountants in Yemen,
    how polite they are,
and the   30   British advisors
    out of a cushy job

            while I slowly & carefully
            wipe   .   Paper's a bit
            on the slick side .

Alicante, March 8, 1968

39

RITUALS PREPARATORY TO THE VOYAGE

"How cum you don' call on me no more?"

No answer's simple.
Friends in this town I've seen
broken bread with, others
not called, not seen, not broken
with either, just the time and weather   .   Spring in
Paris many weathers, hot
& muggy 2 days ago, yesterday spit rain,   the
threat ignored, Bill, Teresa, the kids & I took
lunch to the Bois de Boulogne,   scored, i.e.

The rain held off .
getting hard .

"Pic-nic!" Pound snorted,
Charles reported .

Taking pictures, *pelota*, and wine
white with the sandwiches and cheese.

Eric & Shirley, not called, the
Jonquières not called . Joan's
mother's in town, I wouldn't please her mother . No

rocka da boat, Gil,   "gimme
the smoke, fucka
the world, outa the
blue, singa the song"

RIGHT!

And now to Italy, Spain, maybe
see the old man & talka with him
before he kicka the bucket

No, Ez, no pic-nics.

It's just the time, friends, lovers, master, ladies,
after Easter   /   and the weather

This morning we woke to raining hard
me sweating and apart as you can
get in that sleeping bag
with my early morning kidney-trouble
jiggle-jiggle

Pull on clothes, half-a-block to go
to the nearest vespasienne
        sed my red hen,   ''It's time
        & the sky is falling''

                    Paris rain   .

All the clocks are kicking my keister
south, my balls and my penis   .   Goodbye Paris,
hell-o, Barcelo-
na, hello Venice!

                                    Apr 22. 68

PEEING ALL OVER THE PE-NINSULA : APRIL 1968

At the front of the truck with the door open
or at the back, against the wall,
or into the canale   if there aren't
too many trucks loading too many dorys
wood, mineral water, antiques, empty coke bottles

>   You have to watch the clock
>   on this dock, if
>   the toilets are open and you have the muscle necessary
>   you get that far, but
>   the truth of the matter (excuse the ex-
>   press-
>   ion, is
>   a man gets to where he can and then
>   goes.
>   Right there.

And after one has mucked up the port long enuf:

>   ''Excuse me sir, signor, which way is Rome?''

>   ''Excuse me, sir, signor, all roads lead there.''

>   ''Molto grazie—danke sehr.''

                    □

Too many days in this city
It's gotten down to routines
I try to vary
them .
The usual and unavoidable one starts
when the dock is still empty, 3-4:30 AM .
Take care of the simplest pressures in the canale, then
after a cigarette crawl
back into the sack for a few hours more sleep .

An official rising about 6:30 or 7. Gather
my shaving kit and head for the bar or the port johns.
If it's the UOMINI (next door to
the DONNE, of whom I've seen not a one use the facilities in 10 days)
and take care of the private sector of the morning immediately.
Then coffee and croissant. And washup.

>   If the trattoria/bar, it means I can wait
>   a bit, buy breakfast first, then
>   use their facilities in proper order

42

(they have a mirror).
      Shit, shave, and brush teeth (SIX WEEKS
since I've had a shower), and I'm ready for
serious work.
                         Cross the parking lot to the
camper, turn its furniture from a bedroom into
a sitting/room-studio, spread the serape on the table,
set up the typewriter, then letters, poems, revisions,
translations, some
                         kind of activity. One cup of wine.

Around 9, lower the roof, pack and lock up;
then the boat into town, *accelerata* to
Rialto if I feel slow, *diretto* to San Marco
if I want speed.
                 At Rialto, I always
check the Fermo Posta in case they've
stupidly sent it there, then walk across
the island to San Marco and cold old American Express   .   I ordered
money a week ago from Geneva
and the last three days
I've been, as they say,
expecting.
      The young man is very polite as he tells me: "Nothing." Smiles.

In the calle dei Fabri there's a wineshop

    VINI   .   STELLA D'ITALIA   where
I buy a quarto di vino bianco, a big fat
glass of white for consolation.

                  All this part of the routine is
                  fairly   .   unavoidable.
                  I drink and write, or
                  drink and improve my Italian.
                  Then the possibilities open:
                         10:30 perhaps.

I go to catch a *traghetto*
to Pound's side of the city, San
Gregorio, Santa Maria della Salute.
If they're in, we talk or read or go for a walk,
if not, I
walk, take pictures, take my lunch alone .

                  Today I vary it by
                  going out to the Lido to swim .
                  Salami and cheese and bread I buy
         and a bottle of grappa will last me several days
         and walk out past the hospital where still they've

43

fucked up the beach with *gabinetti* but you don't have to pay .
And after arranging the towel and the food and
lie down on my back and sweat for a bit, I swim.
My first full entry this year into the Mediter-
ranean, water's shallow, so I walk out slow, and when
      a wave gets me waist-deep, bigod, I giggle,
          then dive . eat and sleep .

At 3, I walk my cheap sunburn
              back to the *vaporetto*,
              what's happened is
I've really tricked myself into a hot bath,
the first since the end of March.
I've spotted some public baths some ten
minutes from the parking lot . I dump
my beach gear at the truck and pack fresh towel
some soap, my shaving kit, toothbrush and go
buy me a hot tub for 30 ¢—even wash my hair,
shave, trim hair and beard and moustache, I
find I'm singing . Wash the tub, it's a ring,
what a ring! Not so much a ring as
a one-man bathtub Mafia . incredible. I
keep singing .

          Coffee at Poggia's, then a small
Forst beer (shades of Merano rise, you've nothing to
lose but your alcoholic content) back to the truck,

work . drink . sleep

Smeared head to toe with coldcream, I fall asleep.
The variant strain is taking already. I wake
at 4 AM as usual, but the East is red, red with dawn, and the
trucks are four lines deep already by the dock, tho no boats yet.
It'll be another hot day . Maybe the luck today

will break the bank

and the check will come .   And tho I'm ½ hour late
        all along the line, it does. And I take the
        ¼ de *vino bianco* to

        celebrate.

Late and late again, I
find you can buy wine here *suelto*, i.e.
   bring yr / own bottle.

But the money's here,
well, back in the saddle!

RITUAL XVII.   it takes an hour

Money seems to avoid me in
some mysterious way

                                    so,
                    what else should I do, waiting
                    for my check to be cashed but
use a large Hispano-Olivetti and its outsized carriage
sitting in the middle of the floor

First, tho, they
recognized me from similar occasions, the
check had some kind of stamp across its face, and they
said I had to open an account   .
                                                OKay,
so I agreed I would open an account, if I had to, why not?
Then draw out most of the money, right?

I had the account almost open, all those
questions & answers & signatures, I was even
enjoying it, the
chica filling out the forms filled out a
pretty tight sweater herself, good
legs and lovely breasts resting lightly
                on the desk as she bent
                    her forms

                            to those forms   .   Then,
this damned vicepresident comes back to tell me he'd
got permission to pay me cash, I tried to look grateful .

So she tore up all that paper and I had to
settle for a nice smile and the bust measurement instead of a good,
solid, banking relationship .
But they weren't thru with me yet :

Had to sign it twice myself (*por
motivo de turismo*, that horror), then
the vicepresident, then a clerk, then
another official of some sort, the whole
damned check is covered with signatures, passport No.
addresses, verifications
                        : then I wait
                            some more .

The authorization arrives back   .   even then, the
window of *varios pagos* takes   3   people ahead of me .

45

So I sit and write the first poem I've ever written in a bank .

It   IS   a lovely typewriter, and a handsome type   .   perhaps
I should come here to write
                            all my poems .

June 1968

A SHORT, COLORFUL RIOT POEM FOR LEE MERRILL BYRD

Blue
bottles are blue, green
glass is green .
The West tastes like the North
The South tastes like blood and shit
and magnolia .
I think I can stand it

It is the strength in the arms
you feel
if you lift it

Europe even worse than the States
the price of kleenex, *boucliers*
and tear gas
paving stones and fire
the same clubs

Cream no longer rises to the top, the
perfection of the centrifuge .
A brown unglazed jar.
The flowers are white
with centers green and yellow
how you, fella .   the stone
and broken fingernails, it
is the strength you feel
back and arms
when you lift it, mes copains

If you lift it .
The blottolub,
          the cremaris .

June 1968

16 . VI . 68

Soft, warm, sad, wet
day . Leaving again . Shall
it be the middle of the border?
Vich, Ripoll, and Puigcerda, or
from Ripoll cut off toward Col d'Aret?

> La Junquera's closed by striking agri-
> cultural workers . Nobody mentions Port Bou
> and Cerbère . Get in and drive, you clown .
> I wish I thought the French deserved a
> revolution, or that it were
> from the Pyrenees on down .

THE TOUCH

The windows
are never wide enuf .

Calle del Vidrio, Barcelona, is
off Fernando, toward the Plaza Real;
short, tight, narrow, &
            leads toward the palmtrees

The corner bar to the left is
three to five pesetas cheaper than
the one to the right
            as you enter, plenty of
sky, trees, a fountain, the
            arcades sit over each side we
sit with gambas, cervezas, dis-
cuss my sis-   MARISCAS
ter's imminent   PERCEBES
arrival, I face   ALMEJAS VIVAS
the walls, cannot see   CENTOLLOS
the palmtrees behind me   Y
                                            GAMBAS
                                            ALAJILLO
            BEBA COCA COLA   SEPIA
                                            PULPITO
            BAR   FARAON

                        it says

A quieter day
than yesterday
at the Glorieta, we
sat at the old man's tables in the
back, yesterday, asked
where he was, vacation?
            No, the other waiter says, he's
dead, came into work on a Thursday
didn't come Friday or Saturday,
Saturday died.

An incredible sadness .
You do not have to know these people's
            names to love them, the way
                  the old man moved
                  among the tables, an
                  organized waddle that
cared for so many, so quickly, the new

49

young man works the same station like
a beheaded chicken, no cool to lose, he
whips it out, everything very organized, but
　　　　　it doesn't make the same
　　　　　　　　coherence.　Our friend
's tables are full in the front so we
speak only
when he has time　.　None of us
knows anyone else's name　.

What was he called, the old man?
A gentleness and efficient waddling is
dead now. We do
not need to know
their names to recognize
a pleasure in feeding people well,
　　　　　that rare intimacy, how
miss someone whose name you've never known?
We do not need to know their names, they
minister to us for tips and love they
give is given back. The old man
worked the back—four tables only
in the front—sometimes five, it
depended on how heavy the clientele
was that day.　Today, we
take the full cubierta the first time　.

Again　.　The *viejo* lost to time　.
We never know one another's names, tho
we touched each time　.
I'd come back to Barcelona again
he'd come and touch my shoulder, even
　　　　　if I were not at his tables.　We

do not need to know

anybody's name

to love them.

June 1968

JULY 16, 1968 : AUSTRIAN TYROL

Morning in which
I can keep nothing
hid back
under the green rain
in the green grove
by the green lake in
this green morning under the mountains .

Austrian Alps full of
green stones, kitsch architecture, shit, grüss Gotts,
Germans, Dutch, Swedes, a funny
green morning summer lull, pull and
                love . And

                the flashlight works.

VAUCLUSE

A track? Well yes,
& better than that .
the dignity of a dirt road
leading uphill and
full of rocks .

      Three turns
you can make in second
if you start fast enuf from the
pavée at the bottom . The fourth
you jus gotta shift down to first, one
smooth fast movement inside the bumps,
inandout / the clutch, very fast & smooth .

The machine claws its way up the final slope.
Don't relax yr eye or yr foot's
pressure on the gas pedal
maintain speed   as the signs used to say in the tunnels

     right up that slope where there's a break in the
     stonewall to your left . the eye & foot . now swing
     fast and left   into the small field
                     made it?

     relax yr foot, shift back, f you feel like it,
     to second . move into second, swing to park
     below most of the roofs of the town, the cliffs
     the church . It ain't where the buffalo roam, but
     back in neutral without a stall, you're
     at Cortázar's place, Saignon .

Oscar
Peterson
does Ellington
The Hill of Poetry sits and looks at the valley
                    hills of Haute-Provence
        Mont Ventoux
                    still under snow
                                        June's end .
Summer seen thru browned glasses
is a richness . I
watch her
            haircurlers & slacks
                ironing my slacks, shirts

                                .
                                    My sister
also in curlers
makes deviled eggs   .   My friend
types in another room, his wife
makes *empanadas* for lunch .
Everybody doin his thing . her thing . the

Green and brown of valleys I see behind me now
        red roofs, thru
the tiny blinds and one corner of my
                glasses,
                    great shapes of shaded light
broken by the
earpieces,
thru which show
                            STONE

        ☐

This whole afternoon
hangs itself on insects   .   In the truck
taking afternoon siesta, it was flies.
Outside later, translating under the trees, it was
flies, horse-flies, a bee, two
wasps   .   I work until 10 of 8, when
the first sound of mosquito cracks
thin in my left ear .

        ☐

        All morning work, translating
                at the kitchen table. Two
coffees, three slices bread-and-jam, a beer .   Some

three-quarters thru, quick
voices outside the door of another room,
the *maestro* and the *patron* in the frontyard,
 rattling French
   get to me in their rhythms :
one low and insistent, the other higher and hard,
some impatience there, break my own .

I stop
 rise
    take a book of Gary's poems and go
     out
      up the steps and also
       sit in the sun, and
the wind blows the voices away down in the frontyard .

Up here with the pail of garbage I've moved from the kitchen
slow stages to the dump, there's
     wind
     in the fruit trees, flies,
   wasps buzz happy with the sun after yesterday's rain,
last night's wind, butterflies, can hear
     only buzz and birds
and wind, apricot, peach, figtrees, bees in the gladiolas,
   a hummingbird in the hollyhocks
   flies in the vine leaves,
the voices
blown away
down this valley, clouds
stretch, towns shine, a
light brown under sun
a book of poems for the hand, other
rhythms for the mind .
 buzz .
 work .

  not done

  ☐

  Because I have left the door open
  there is always a matter of insects
  the wind in these high valleys blows
   in . I
have to take a butterfly out in my hands before he
batters himself to death against the
glass pane
between the living room and the kitchen .

Then a wasp discovers the fruit bowl in the corner.

He checks out the oranges and the mayonnaise jar
and settles on the bruised portion of a pear . O, yes!
        Lemons
        peaches
        a melon
            but returns to
                            the bruised pear its
                            speckled skin, he
hovers and sucks, he checks my outgoing mail,
my empty pastis glass, the story now translated,
even the lines of this notebook where he walks

        for a bit, but returns

        makes love to the pear .

THE SAIGNON SUITE

THE SLOPE

Looking up the hill
toward the town, thinking:
the mailman,
telephone call to be made, the
garbage .

BEFORE LUNCH

Cortázar in shorts, that length
stretched along the walk a fair piece,
in the sun . in an hour
un apéritif!

THE DUMP

As you put it
in, over the high fence-boards
one lower edge of the village, the cats
leap out !!   disappear
in several directions . wait .
watch you .

SUPPER OUTSIDE

The buzz of wasps be now
over the plates on the table
under the fruit trees .

TANKS

Houses three stories high
or block homes of apartments
    both with steep Norman roofs

The fish swims in the river
and shares it with other fish
        The cabbages have a garden
        to share with the lettuce and radishes,
            the tomatoes

The cow has a small pasture
and grazes it by herself

            An old man lies on a sack on
            a hillside in the sun
            after lunch .
            watches the train whip by

The dead lie in the cemetery near the tracks
share earth with the other dead
and do not look at anything

A barge on the river barges past, the wash flying
The fish swim in the river
        They share it with the barge,
           the fishermen .

The end of a distance come
so early in the morning
      where the eye stops,
                             flames
running   O   their tongues up thru
    along the rooftree of
        down the coping of
            that church in Harlem .

DRIVING RAIN
wind driving a winter rain and fire, O
the twigs stripping outside the classroom window
we watch sexy

anything

      vegetable, tall and branched
              yellow, the fire
              yellow, the leaves
              yellow, the girl's blouse
grey, the slacks
grey, the day outside
grey, smoke rising pierced by flames

      turning blue to red to yellow
         which leads to a discussion of
the personal character of firemen and cops, not
altogether complimentary
      but granting courage   .   A Harlem precinct
      hd/bn firebombed earlier that morning .
Where the eye stops
smoke and flames thru the hill's trees, their
branches stripping . burning the whipping rain
         inscrutable cracks . Whaddya hear?
      The blindman singing on the uptown train
coins in the enamelled metal cup clink

She sits back in the desk no longer thinking

a dreamy look on her face :
                    "It is so pretty," she says .
Her yellow blouse sighs up and down
The rain strips the branches, drives the
                    fire across the church roof
                    where the eyes stop.

                    ⊡

Smoke floats
          in its layers upon
                    the room's air   .   has
                    nowhere to go . floats
MALIK   is   king   .   King is dead of assassin's bullet
Malik is dead of assassin's bullet
Three Kennedys down and one to go .

Dallas is in Texas
California one might have suspected
and Memphis is on the river
and the Audubon Ballroom at 167th Street
belongs to the CIA under prior contract
          Two cats move in the sunlight
          stream thru the window
          wash, kiss, wrestle, play
          under the smokehaze   .   they
          are black cats   .   Yoruba, what
does Oshun mean?   Ouan Jin, or the
     man of education?

Feet raised in sunlight
against the other's face
          King dead
          Malcolm dead
w h o   w i l l   b e   t h e   n e x t   t o   g o ?
     Ted?
          And then she married Onassis,
          a prescient woman, to the
          Eastern Mediterranean, this time .
You have to transport the stuff
He has the boats . He passes .
          My friend, Economou, a medievalist
          and poet, owns the most spec-

tacular Afro I've ever seen. The
people pass him in the street and speak to him,
   "Hello, brother." He refuses to pass.
                               But Onassis?
and Jack the Cowgirl?
They pass everywhere, it
                   is a conspiracy between
East and West .   what
   did you think Bouvier meant?
         The sunlight goes .
It is a clear light from the South
smogged in . The cats sit
           and wash themselves
              in the window
                 look out .
What did you think Bouvier meant?

Gassir's lute
   The light
     shining on Oshun's face
     is not easy to behold . to be held .
Do you think you can put your hat on your head
and walk away with him?   Down that hill?
    But Haarlem is a Dutch name
    and the Dutch have forgotten us . Deutsch?
The destroyer?   What did you think Oshun meant?
Ogun,
Yoruba is his tribe
The six powers of light
The sunlight across the window, Hooo
Dierra, Agada, Ganna, Silla, Hooo Fassa!
       Wagadu the legendary city of the Fasa .
The epic Dausi goes back to   500   perhaps BC, at
         which time Homer . The
remnant of that tribe, mostly Muslim, holds
two desert oases . Tichit and Walatu . The blood
of seven of his sons
    dripped
over his shoulder
onto his lute
to feed the song .
        or John?

"I dig
   talking to a black man   who
   thinks of a white man
   as just another kind of black man."

OR vice versa,
OR thank you, Leo Frobenius
                    —to feed the song .

               □

Elaine calls me at 3 A.M. from Toronto. I come up out of a
deep dream, furious. No one else calls me at three in the morning.
I've been sick for two days now. I yell at her and wish her a
happy birthday. Nothing is such a pain in the ass as being
loved where one does not love : it is
an humiliation for both parties
Elaine is just such a pain in the ass. She says
we are married in her dream. I must say she has better
dreams than I do. I'm dreaming of an absolutely natural hair, a
single, intricately curled, long, brown hair in a tiny plastic
container you can see thru like a fuse, loose at both ends, beautiful-
ly involuted and fine. This is an absolutely indispensable item
in a list of objects which must be collected, this wild hair in its
artificial little glass tomb, carefully random, carefully natural .
An absolute fake essential to the collection, essential for a
correct life.

The Ft. Moultrie flag on a recent 6¢ stamp
is the word   LIBERTY   toward the bottom
across a ground of dark blue, and in the upper lefthand corner,
the last quarter of a waning moon . PIE IN THE SKY .
Ft. Moultrie is in Charleston, South Carolina .

The black cat comes and sits directly on the notebook
in which one is trying to write a poem
It is not that she does not know, but will not
confront you eye to eye, sits and looks in another direction
upon your papers.   And purrs.

     All right, Elaine, get off my back.
I pick the cat up and put her down on the floor
     & go on.
            And it doesn't stop.   None
of it stops, ever,   it needs that wild hair in its
            plastic container, the essential image . So .

                61

I stay up until dawn reading Philip Whalen's first book
    which after all these years still turns me on .

          ⊡

    "You goin'ta tell me I
        hafto give up
            mah *piece?*"

THE TREES

Leaves on the branches
At the end of branches twigs
carrying everything
brushing against each other
reachingtoward everything
touching everything   .   The air.

A spooky green wheel
    with spokes that move
        like a stagecoach in the movies
           and a star
                all of it green,   face
the eye of my friend Kelly at his desk
: a map of southwest Asia which cuts short
somewhere in the middle of Burma and
an element chart   the 103 blank space, a gift
      of   THE ATOMIC DEVELOPMENT MUTUAL FUND, W.C., a
map of ancient Greece with a lot of the islands unmarked,
feathers and pens
two packs of camels, postage stamps, a scarab—no
a scorpion sunk in violet plastic, violently .
      2   bottles of Pelikan Tusche, a bottle
marked: Spiritus vini Root Purissimus

    a plastic tube of fat pills from

Caldor   of Kingston, Inc. 31817 . 11/27/68
            for Robert Kelly, Bard College
            One every four hours for
            pain

and a lot of books—

DECEMBER JOURNAL : 1968

December 13, 1968 .

A saturday-seeming sunlight in the front room
    the quieter pace   .   I do many pickup chores
        without pressure & quickly   .   tho
           it is only friday

Two black cats sit on the dirty couch & observe me reading,
drinking my coffee, first of the day . They are waiting for me
to feed them.

I came back from the telephone and got into bed in the cold room.
The covers were still warm. She was raised on her left elbow,
looking at me . It wasn't fear, nor acceptance, nor anticipation.
The cusp of necessity. I stroked her hair a few times and told her:

"Your father is dead." Her hair is long & black & fine,
her head rounded underneath it, under my stroking hand.   It breaks,
falls against my chest, my shoulder suddenly wet with tears .
Sobs come openly from the throat, not choked back, neither opened
to scream . I hold her hand, continue stroking.   I wish she cd/
scream. I wish I cd/ .

ROAR

The cats sit together on the bathmat near the door & observe me
sitting on the pot . first of the day . They
are waiting for me to feed them.   I clean their box.
In the front room, one sits in the single spot of sun on the floor,
                                    the other
climbs the wooden louver, swings up to the top as the blind
swings with her weight, rides it to the centersash . sits there .

The shaft of light falls across my legs, belly & lower chest, cock
& balls lie softly in the shadow of this notebook, shadow
of the pen follows the line across the page, mixed with
the shadow of my hand moving, the shadow of the
cats on the arm of the sofa, ear-and-whisker shadows

Shadows .

"My two grandfathers accompany me."

I hold her and she weeps for a long time. We are naked and
alone in the world, lie there as one, and one and two, I hold her
and we sleep. for an hour.

Warm & desolate under the blankets in a cold room
in another man's house   /   in Annandale, New York
           somewhere in time

                                .

                        sleep.

Wake.
Telephone calls . when is the wake?   telephone calls, red eyes,
red nose, put on clothes . coffee (hostess descends) eggs
in a savory omlet . juice . more coffee . books . host
is raised and lowered
                  EAT OF MY FLESH, DRINK OF MY BLOOD

The host descends . The chalice of coffee is a milkcan half full
           : a large man . Joan and I
           have finished the Fundador (drink of my blood)

[Thou shalt live forever . . .

                        Gone
                        under .
                        or
                        above?

The mind travels among the stars . we in this prison earth
           await our time
           "It is necessary for the conservation of the universe
for each thing to desire & demand the perpetuation of its kind."
                  Joan has ours in the oven cooking (heaven?)
                        awaits her time .

[Osiris lies in the sunlight on a copy of *IO*, the
Alchemical Issue, open to Kelly's journal   . Ablutions.]

                        Coffee . 3rd cup . The Sky

The chemicals of
an industrial society
mitigate the sky over East Seventh Street, Manhattan . Colors

           "If you have dissipated & lost the greenness
                              of the Mercury
& the redness of the Sulphur, you have lost

                        65

the soul of the stone.''

fade .

Isis leaves the third shelf down of the large bookcase
and tries the louvers again . her weight
swings them back in this time,
makes the ascent impossible impossible,
however she
studies the problem, then sits on top
of the sewing machine & cries.

(I hold her against me & we both sleep)

''Every chemical agent requires a prepared material;   it is
for that reason that a man absolutely cannot breed
with a dead woman.''

The plants are dying.
I do not give them water.

METALS
LIVE

I let them die.
I have to go out and buy

new plants, a new
planting .

Stone already knows the form
of the statue within it.

S T O N E

People arrive for talk.
There is talk. Joan
talks again on the telephone. Red eyes,
red nose in a chalk face.   We
hold one another in the bathroom upstairs
in the hall by the stairwell.   Excuse ourselves,
go out to walk in the cold December day.
Drive first to Blithewood . park . walk about
the Zabriskie estate, down thru the formal garden

OUT   THE   DOOR

into the field, slopes
down, toward the Hudson, around the cold, walled
garden, back

66

                        the opposite side, walk
arm-in-arm up the steps like any funeral or
marriage, drive two minutes another road . park.

    walk down past the swimming pool, along the small
rushing river, two falls, a couple coming toward us whom
we greet, a boy & girl, who climb back the way we have come

IT IS MIRRORS

We walk down

they have come
to the river
        (we have
against the cold sun
under the trees . hands held . looking out upon the flatness.
A skinny island runs thru the middle . railroad tracks .
    We cannot see the other side
        of the river . this low altitude . Water & sun.
Shells of water chestnut underfoot
    four-horned & light . seeds inside .
    Two in the drawer of my telephone stand now
    in the front room . bullheads . Osiris sleeps in my lap .
    Seeds inside . His head turns against the notebook.
        The plants die . their screams
            fill the room . Reflected sun
against the church walls across the street . Two
watertowers, the bulb-shaped steeple of orthodoxy, the
    triple-cross of Russia

SEEDPODS

    "Have the greatest care, lest the blackness appear twice;
once the little crows have flown away from their nest, they
can never come back again."

The mind travels among the stars . we
in this prison earth   await our time

AWAIT HER TIME

The King, naked but for his crown
sits reclining in a large basket, an oil
lamp burning on the basket wall to his right, the basket
open on top and on the king's left side, a kind
of showcase orgone box . On the stone floor beneath it
a fire is laid . smoke rises .
he is burning his ass off in an orgone accumulator
          It is a cremation?   Creation?

          □

She ran down the slope in Central Park that summer night,
I right behind her, caught her round and threw her down
It is a hillside, the earth under us .
     We walk back up thru the light rain
          to her parents' apartment to
               dry one another off . to fuck.
                    She will never tell me her real name.

                    "Colored lights, it is colored lights,
                         most of it going to purple & violet,"
                              is all she will say . We
do not ask each other for love
     we just take it . and thrash
about in the bed of her father and mother . far away
     the sound of rain, tires on wet streets, who is it
        having the vacation? She
               will not tell me her real name,
                    turns into a tree .

          □

I will not speak of the driving
in silence, silences of speed . the parkways of the mind
swift barren trees . She is filled
     grief & life . I had to
roll her over me to the outside of the bed that morning,
to get her up, found it was myself
had gotten up . fucked her . right there .

A morning after that, after the first night of wake,
she had bought the ring entire, said, at twenty to eight,
     "You have to get up and move the car."

I existed again, I
was married to my wife!

who was mourning her dad,
awaiting her time . life
in her belly . the way
we must be, a posture of a single
oneness, the beast in the bed.
O my baby!

The sun is yellow & pale, not red, these last mornings, I
drive very fast.

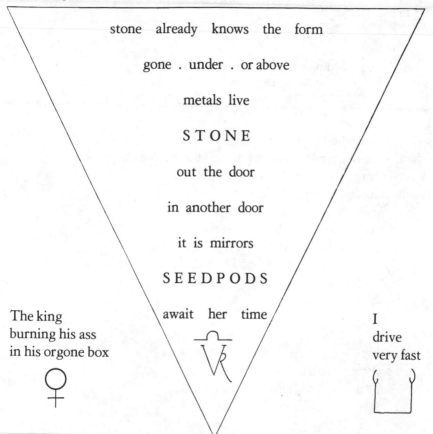

stone   already   knows   the   form

gone . under . or above

metals live

S T O N E

out the door

in another door

it is mirrors

S E E D P O D S

await   her   time

The king
burning his ass
in his orgone box

I
drive
very fast

Sitting on the ashtray, ''Yes,
I've been here be-fore''

reading about caterpillars, bees, wasps, (*les guêpes*)
that were my friends, Saignon-par-Apt in the Vaucluse, last summer;
old Fabre at his *harmas* at Serignan,

setting down the days:

''The common wasp and the Polistes
are my dinner-guests: they
visit my table to see if the grapes served
are as ripe as they look.''

And half-a-year has gone,
and Joan swells patiently and smiles, not from wasp-stings .
And I sing in this hotel room in Boquerón
which has no proper ashtray, so must
use the john, I sit hereon, reading
and smoking . Hot ash or the butts themselves,
hiss as they are dumped. Sitting on
the ashtray—do I have to pee or dump?
I do. Never move except to wipe,
or flush .

Sunburnt
from this Caribbean island's heat, it is
last summer's sun is in the mind :
pastis at 11, Julio's sunbathing done .
recreation, translation, shop in Apt .
Les guêpes
still stir in my head . I have seen them here
in Boquerón, in the grasses,
lazing about in the poinsetta bush with the butterflies .
Une autre saison, un autre monde, another year .
still I sit . *Quand même,*
Julio caught one in his armpit, last summer,
between the shortsleeved shirt and the long hairs,
to the panic and discomfort of them both . O
the Hymenoptera, what we shd/   fear!

□

The gnat-whine, a twin-motor overhead:
circles widen from where the small fish
surface for an instant ,
                    The beercan
                    floats peacefully

            ''out in the tranquil bay''

Catches the flash of sunlight, drifts
                    with the tideturn toward
the white and orange of the dock's Gulf sign .

                              Boquerón, P.R. Dec / Jan

PUERTO RICO

Seaplane going over, going
     somewhere . over
         head, the blue re-
            ally re-
                    flected in this sea .

See
the dust of the street, see
the beach . A bitch to listen
to .
Lie there and listen to waves, gulls, other
more spectacular but soundless birds .
Boquerón . The sun
is harsh and ethereal . One man
stands on a balcony watching
another man . among
the TV aerials .

The birds dive
to live .

There is an irregular movement of the light and

                        all things are changed
                        new and old
                        past & not yet born
                        enter it
                        as one

Cannot keep my heart
as bright
as this spring is

                Lady Godiva on a chopped hog
                makes it new

          ⊟

Muscles bend it
to the face to
face . no turning now, the very way of knowing,
                        renewing

"I want her hands on my back
                    tho that not be possible"
has been a blue flowering plant of mine,
the most of a year now.

                Limonium commune californicum

woody root (that's mine!) leaves obovate-
to oblong-spatulate, obtuse,
or sometimes retuse, tapering
below into a rather long petiole, 4-9 inches long;
calyx lobes membranous at tip, I'm hip,

                    corolla violet-purple

a deeper shade of
blue, the closer
I git   to   limonium commune californication

                ⊞

Eastern window, so
sun on my eye brings
me upright in bed, 7 AM
or so . I go

to the phone when it rings
petals of fire =
ize the positions .

                    "Salt marshes and sea beaches
                    along the coast, Los
                    Angeles County to Humboldt County,
                    July to December"
                                        Jepson sez.

Tho April only
by noon, let us see, what we
can bring to
blossom here this city by the Bay, or
once more, Saxifrage, flowers perfect,
perigynous, usually white, often red,

            never blue .
                    "Seed with endosperm"
                                        Jepson sez.
Ole!
        an irregular movement of the light
                        and all things
                    move beneath it and
                            are changed .

73

Muddiness
    of the Columbia River in spring :
on takeoff . a springoff south .

        One wonders when it began
        what it looks like there in time
        We know our sources.
        I know what I have drawn from you this time

Can see the mountains below
still under snow
The Pacific to my far right
  fades into fogs .

Have seen you as woman longer than
you, yourself have, wonder now at the tenderness
as we walk about the grass at yr / wedding reception, smoking
grass upon the grass, yr / hips moving gently, that
        between them all men prize
          blind their eyes—

Keep the Sierras out the window to my left, the
Pacific to my right, the plane comes down, San
Francisco . How
keep any of it down, it all keeps rising .
Matt Helm is a dirty old man who can't get it up
      —white flesh—
    he needs all that whisper around him
Speak to Dino about it, he knows.

Eldridge is Soul . Eldridge study
        karate, man, the true prez
photographed on the cover of his
        book on love,
        Soul On Ice,
        sing that twice,
holding cala lilies
for the tomb, man, of all that
                Whiteness.

I read his book on the transcontinental Pan Am mutherfucking
plane, man, &
weep at the beauty of it
soul, right there, the tears go down
for all the hopeless love I've spent in my life
I'm a baby . I write pomes . I say
"Look at me, see what I can do?"
  I feed me on it . And weep
    the beauty of all our loves
     across mid America
      looking down, man,
all those clouds,
those white clouds . all that white
shit down there .
What you don't see
unless you see
through .

     (Over New Jersey,
   you can see the real estate from the air)
Cape May:
The American coastline cuts away to the left.
The left wing of the plane dips
   the turn . North, now .

PLANS AND CHIPS

The three
trees on the corner square

          stand up
          & call to you

The two
lights on the doorway across the street

          5 A.M.
          shine in & are
          my eyes

Birds outside
cheer up, how
can I say—sing?

     See? Carlos T.
     chirrups in his crib, quiet
          after long screaming

I'm going to
die, I'm afraid . O-
kay, I'm afraid, I
shall hold you in Front Royal, Ashville,
Nashville, Memphis, Springfield, Alamosa,
     Aspen even, Rawlings, Boise, Portland,
          other towns to the South .

Our asses, our mouths.

A DIFFERENT POEM

Stay with me
sway with me
going up that road
looking back

        the green on either side
        trees, the green between
        the sounds

mad houses
mad streets
mad loves
mad mice or roaches
madmen

     spurting love
     streaming songs
     petting kittens
     stroking seashells

Sunshine, I
long for any moment of peace, a cat
quiet paws below the trajectory
        of seagulls crying
          garbage dumps
            for breakfast

some dry cereal
some coffee, hell, what is it
      any of us need—touch?
Love is no groove, love and simply catch
a path of talk
a patch of green either side, walk
     down it, swaying   (sway with me)
        in the drunken dawn, I
          feed you, I
          need you,
     how can I tell why

stay near you ever out of great fullness

        solitude,
        both our minds?

      Flesh come home, I
      seed you, it

flies like a gull
soars like a sound
runs like a dog or horse, runs
away, swift stalking like a cat
under cars, between buildings, down
       slope among the grasses .

Did the animal die?
Is it lost & hungry somewhere?
Did it run away? What
       did it find . I mean
       it's both our asses, I
       can ask, can't I?

Tangle of sheets in the backroom;
tableau with no sheet in the front :

    G. & E. heavy in the backroom
                      snarl of whites

    Joan in the front, a 5-week-old Carlos
    hangs from her front by suction . all asleep .
                        I hang
out the window 5:30 A.M., 7th Street dawn.

        The sealpoint Siamese kitten got
itself locked out in the hall last night, wanted
    into the closet, probably . By
this morning everyone in the house
    must have heard him screaming .

The stairway in the ruins wanders up to a
windswept third floor, the stone keeps
    worn to a ——⌣—— in the middle .
An aluminum handrail ruins the take & makes
the perspective, 700-odd-years later where
            once was a wall . Peire Vidal
    had fallen heavily against it, his way back
from that lovely bitch in the kitchen to his honored room
above, carrying his britches, to sleep alone in his shirt
sodden with wine to dream of that noble bitch in Marseille,
Barrals' wife, his own true love, the kiss he'd snatched
that morning, her lord out riding, not giving a damn except
for Vidal's weird conversation & the master singer's voice
& that the port run well, it did, but his priggish wife
took care of that, raising such a stink that he had to
(sternly) suggest to Vidal a prolonged absence, so
where did the fool go?
          to her brothers in the hills back of
    Marseille, Guillem and Uc Les Baux . The lady'd been
born in that castle, Alazais de Rocamartina, against the rock
wall, the light falls against
    Vidal falls heavily against it, damn the wine, light
    but catches up to you, stands a moment, what was it

Uc had said? en Richart . . . another crusade . . . that's
the ticket, Coeur de Lion would keep his throat damp
with the light Rhône wines, by damn, over the sea it
would be, overseas, forget the stolen kiss, forget . . .
                    another few steps, falls again

The stone stays
        The shadow moves
The songs stay, too, mostly unread, un-
sung, tho the language persists
in the village of Les Baux, those hills
stay, the stairway
                                        where the feet have worn it .

                □

Family . 2 black cats & token whitey

        gather in the window,

                            look at the street .
The Gaucelm Faidit Uzerchemobile at the curb, the
family upstairs, double-park their Dodge, put the
trunk together for the Jersey beaches, pic-nic, getting
                            an early start
                            6 A.M.
        The father fat & bald and somewhat
        nervous (beats his wife when necessary,
        smokes too much); the boy, the youngest,
also much too fat at   12   a golden
crown of curls, alert, piggish eyes
sees the family of cats first, watching them, speaks:
            "Hey, look!" The daughter
                            where the waters run
            a 16-yr-old, shapely mass
of eyeglasses, tooth-braces, & shyness (her
best years were between 12 and 14), that
second bloom yet to come, asks up:
        "Did you find the cat in the hall?"

        I nod, smile, hold
        up the kitten who yells.
Her mother I've had fantasies about for years,
one of the best figures of any married woman in the block
a body that takes the beatings, grows the kids up, is
too busy packing last-minute things to
even notice, does not look

80

up. I nod to the father, mark the obvious:
"You're getting an early start."
He smiles and answers, then remembers
I do not speak Ukranian, puts it in English.

"It is be a good long day."

The cats check the *gorriones* out, sparrows
of the ledge above, the gutters below .
CHIP .
repeatedly .

Joan stretches her hand & presses
against the wall
her feet search the bunched blanket, bottom of the bed,
like small animals
turns on her side, good legs curled .
Carlos   CHIPS   & dozes again

The long greeen Dodge eases out of the street, I note
that one of the priests
from the orthodox church
across the street
has been using a stretch of sidewalk in front of the church,
turning always, it's a tether, two ends, friends,
the door of the nunnery one side,
the fire hydrant at the other, this side
of the identical-size & color house, serves as a rectory,

uses it
as tho it were
a graveled meditation walk
to read his breviary, glances up
as a young nun comes down the church
steps, having set the altar for morning mass
She
does the steps more quickly, looks away down
the street toward Second Avenue .
A young matron with a broad ass and tight skirt,
short skirt & green, goes up
the steps from the street, 6:15
confession?

I wonder, as the priest folds up his book, hikes
his cassock up with one hand, also
climbs the steps,
goes in by a side door. She

81

is the organist, maybe?
Ends that scene .

In slacks, Sara Penn crosses the street .
The cupola rises green and exotic
above the bell tower .
the hour, 7:15

⊡ 28 . VI . 69

None of the radio stations ╱ in southern Pennsylvania
play programs of marches this Independence Day morning .
I miss my Sousa.

My 'Fairest of the Fair' however
regales our Carlos, breast, bottle & dish.

A full morning .
I wonder if all the Men's in the picnic areas
along 81 South paint the inside walls
of their shithouses black. It's very depressing
just to start with . the roughcut slabs of pine
creosoted & browned on the outside, on the insides
are black, the sloppy brushstrokes showing
against the grain .

So you sit on the luxurious chemical toilets surrounded
by blackness—not so cheerful .

I think I'll request the Pennsylvania Park Service
to paint the inside of their restrooms bright
yellow, so you can see the friendly flies &
spiders, that disappear against
creosote black . A

relief to look up to the inside of the
unpainted roof & see a wasp beginning
her nest, some spider webs .

Sí, señor, HOW TO SEE IS
MY PLEASURE, the

black flies buzz my ass, my
head, I cannot see them .

JULY 21-22 . 1969

Those boys comin back fr / the moon
    Armstrong, Aldrin & company, & I
         make my own countdown :   score
be
tween
dusk & midnite, I
missed one rabbit & got one, I think,
         rear wheels, one small bird, &
also about dusk
    (the small ones do a dance in front of the
              windshield in pairs)
    a young hawk crossed
    right to left &
    cut back

        hit the upper right side
        the VW truck's window
               W H A P
                    & bounced off .
I bet he got a sore belly .
I never before met me a silly hawk
& that was surely just showoff stuff, that
cutting back .
    No point in counting the bugs.

    The small bird I prayed to, he
    protected me later that night .
    I couldn't pray to the rabbit, only
        apologize .

    □

    Springfield (Mo.) to near to Boise City (Keyes)
        OKLA
        HOMA
    500 miles in a day
then Raton, Cimarron, Eagle Nest
    Joan drove those mountains , Raton to
        Taos on 65 . 111 north to Tres Piedras &

83

285 straight up
                into those hills (2 rainstorms,   in the
                        distance lightning) & at La Jara, 14
miles south of our mark, our Car-
los starts
                HOWLING . we stop . feed,
                        walk him around a bit
the driveway where are tanks and sheds, a fertilizer co-op, the
                        final quiet, then
6   miles in toward the San Juan range on Colorado   370, Bobby's
letter sd/ that's   15   kilometers, right?, then another mile
& a "dirty, yellow/brown house"
                        got that, there's
                                no   one   there .

Check the window
        (I peer thru, see books, it's
            the house alright)   door's open
                    inside a cat with a half-moustache
                            talks back . what then?
2   empty bottles of Beam, the water's hot
                    what?
                            we're home
                                    they're not
Another cat arrives later .

We   3
fall asleep .
The cats probably also

                Those other boys too
                comin' in,
                back from the moon .

            □

84

AUGUST JOURNAL   1969

Scrambled in the dark dug of dawn
is warm against the cheek, is
a wet, salty sweetness to the
multiplication table of
mouth .

> Eiaeia-eh
> Eiaeia-eh
> Eia-eia-ng

Find the soft spot where the silence is / is
        a rocking indeed .

☐

      "Wal, thet's a funny lookin jug
          has a hole in it
shaped like a diamond on a playin card .
Think you cn drink outn that?"

☐

Just north of the bar at Arroyo Hondo, N.M., make a right on a dirt road .
As you continue, the road curves gently to the right, pass the store and the
church, a fence begins on one side, the road continues . you do not .
make a left thru that fence, but then take all the choices to your right. up
till you arrive at the top of the mesa . The map is a brown paper bag drawn
back at the bar. There are two six-packs of beer in it . Hardly a fountain
but anyway
a blessing
on a hot day
Three tepees, a trailer that fits on the bed of a pickup truck without the truck,
a small common-house : field to the left full of vegetables, field to the right
an adobe garden : the main house is going up at the far edge of the field to the
right . the clay under your feet, man, is what makes the adobe . Six people.
stripped or partly stripped, are stripping logs, Douglas fir. already cut to
size . Max with his mouth half-full of teeth, smiles when he sees the beer
and me, lined face, hard body, a soft smile . The beer is divided up . two girls
bum me for cigarette, a pleasure to light them up in the strong wind, bending
toward my cupped hands, the firm hang of tits brown in the wind bringing rain.

Twentyfour or five people live there for the summer . The Reality Construction Company, Box 701, it is Max's second commune. An interior strength to surviv an isolated winter on the mesa, a soft man too.

☐

Douglas pines
about the lake

      I have passed many summers without you .

the wind thru them . enormous
comes on the earth beneath them
cones, the stumpy phallus, the fat mind

We are barely in California
      6   miles in, I know, the
      tow truck told me so .

We wait
for days.
     I see
your steamy tits rising in the summer night, the
laugh and crag of yr / face fuzzy
   against the mountain moon-
           light .
Hip-hip   hip-hip
  & Cali-for-ni-yay
     Cones fall .   a dog barks
                   yip-yip .

THEY ARE NOT THE SAME
The panes
of six of the 13 windows in this wheelhouse
are fogged
     just breath & body heat
     this cool morning

          as the berth lies facing north
          sun rises to the starboard side

The gentle motion side to side
keeps just your shoulders & ass moving
gently, cheek to cheek, just to remind you
               water under you . The same
    roll
    triggers Denis Kelly
      to lust for
         roar of the twin motors
yachtsman's cap to top his shaggy head, his belly
           next the wooden wheel
a handgrasp to wooden pins
connects the shaft . a power transmission
a good sea-stride from the gentle motion of the cheeks
above the harbor swell . it is not the same

The gull stands on the piling hits my eye between
the locker shacks on the pier painted a dull identical tan
[consecutively numbered, they are not the same, not
by content or location of door, nor by width of board, nor
how the corner joints are laid and nailed or finished .

Another gull stood on that same pile yesterday, preening,
turning his head about to survey the prospects
                         . water reflects
sun, wavering seaweeds of light against the underpinning timbers
of the pier another sameness always changing, never quite
identical . the same timelessness . it is not the same
gull

"Can you tell one gull from another? They all look the
        gull to me." They are not the same . They all
are beautiful, they are not the same, there
                is difference even in their voices, one
trajectory of dive, level off or swooping patterns cut
thru flight in air, are no two the same gull, feet tucked up.

We sleep while we are waking
o, the easy swell rocks us,
cheek-to-cheek, on timbers of the dock, on the hull of
the boat two berths away, on
ceiling of this cabin where we move
                softly, love, the flicker
        of the net of light and water
where we live
                        changes . ripple glint in the tide turn .
                            it is not the same .

Cold day   & bright sun
wind holding the flags straight out

flap/flap

sound of lines & rigging clicking
against the masts all round us
quiet insistence to ear as reinforcement
to eye . bell buoy beyond in the bay
bounds and bongs

Joan ''does'' her exercises on the center deck
in   bathing suit   in sun, the
handsome legs rising & moving an arc
and falling alternately . cool / warm flesh
bikini for figleaf, goosepimples . smile.

Thus the   3   graces & the   4   dignities;
thus the rules of Ch'an are
maintained
between us

standing

sitting
walking

& lying down.

grace of word,
of deed,
grace of thought

This boat that has no name
but a numbered berth
rolls gently   .   we
look upon one another
& our eyes are at peace .

SEPTEMBER JOURNAL

My friend, Byrd, looks
at a moon just past first
quarter, late July, says:
    "Hey!
You bin stepped on!"   half
    quoting a poem of his .

    □

        In September,
        I bring him back great

chunks of wood from
Idaho . bandsaw-split
Douglas pine . He
& Lee are not here, are
somehow in Tennessee . I
can't see why, but anyway

        like the flocks of birds resting
        on trees fringing this yard, their
        way south, our way east, we
stay a few days . Wind is
cold afternoons, there
        is hard rain .

    □

Between where Interstate 70 ends
        temporarily, all the
     traffic is back to East 40 (2 lanes, be
careful passing)
Teotopolis and Altamont, those towns, Shum-
way, Montrose, Effingham, to Terra Haute

Rest area just off 70, the johns
are in the gas station at a corner across the highway
likewise a farmyard full of pigs . but don't
mention animals : a Penn Central engine roars past hauling
the whole 27 cars of the Barnum & Bailey Circus, plus

one green caboose .

Hang loose, Ed. It's been a good year
Our sons, Carlos & Kid burn
3 months apart .
Barnum & Bailey goes thru

The tender little end-of-summer grasses
move green & ragged in a southern
Illinois wind, will be
under snow soon .

The flies are sluggish on the
fallen leaves .
Warm weather's gone .

Rain   rain, the
                whole damn day,
Hatteras to Montauk
Cape Ann to Casco Bay.

            At Kennebunk now
it still comes down
the thurgling sound in the drains
an extension of the coast to the outer edges of
no beach, that snow leak down
offn trees   .   upper
reaches of the Connecticut River
some other
4 A.M., different winter
different year .

Syracuse a stopoff
en route to Buffalo, Saint
            Patrick's Day . Winter
            still on the land . We
            land   . smoothly.

Roads wind black against snowfields
      Lakes still frozen . large
freeforms of white below . March
17th . ice still holding .

400   cops on the Buffalo campus . two
were fired on yesterday, 2:30 in the morning,
.22 caliber thought sufficient, or
            what we had? . I
take it I am part of the fourth week of chaos
& intermittent violence.   Still holding .

            The ice is .
            You can't go to Cuba yet
            but illegally, but
you *can* get to China if the chinks will give you a visa .
And Agnew, after addressing a private luncheon, yet, of
the Association of Radio and Television News Anal-
            ysts, remarked:
            "I'm talked out."
I'll believe it when I read the seismographic reports.

How do you say "¡Venceremos!" in Chinese?

I travel also
to Buffalo .

AGAINST THE SILENCE OF STAIRCASES

Scrap .
whatwe bindoin' all week . Blow
all of it up . out .
                        down? what
do those steps mean, worn as they are by
centuries of walking up and down
them, literal *u*'s in the center of them . I
ask you, what does my 2nd wife's ass, (fo / to)
pinned to the wall of my workroom, great
generous curves either cheek, rosebush
of hair centering the photograph, the white shirt,
arm fallen over in speechless relaxation,
                mean to you?   Means to me
sleep . curling against it . seen
                much too often . Now

the S U N   shines outside, first today, the rain and
grey gone from the streets .
                Man rides a bicycle
up Hall Place, a drunk crosses on 6th St. totters east, the
S T O P   sign lays its white lettering up against
permanent red . We
can never go away .
                    Don't never
                    go away . Not
                    even in yr / head .

JOURNAL: MAY 1970

These equations work out
no work today . I don't believe it .
Octavio Paz leans back against the fire escape across
the street and waves . I don't believe it .
Hollo is as Hollo does . I don't believe it .
I'm in one helluva doubtful mood this morning .
Peevish, pernicious . A spoonful is
as much as a spoon holds . June holds . Moonholes
where cd we find the tropics if not west of here?
somewhere . let's get hot soon as we cross the border .

Have you seen something comparable?
My friend, I have not .
Ellen, Joan, Eunice, Rosemary, Frances, Barbara, and a
young actress who shit in a bag hung from her waist, which
encompasses that year . There's the kid to show for it, sits
middle of the floor, a milkcarton pendant from his right hand .
The 4th of May. His first
birthday this month . now the empty egg carton's on the floor .
What next? Bottle of vodka knocked over . He dances south, he
crawls east . he
bedaubs himself . Tell me some more .

Okay.

crawl	yawl	
sprawl	mewl	
brawl	owl	
drawl	bowl	
caterwaul		anything else?

prowl	bowl	
growl		
bowel(?)		bowels or Bolles

lives two doors away .
We never could find Memphis . Out
Atlanta! out Nefertiti! Athens
Ohio . Montgomery used to be a friend of mine. Aetna .
Gretna, Virginia . Gloria
still coming down that mountain trail, 11,000 ft. or so,
in shorts .

96

6 A.M.
and it's still dark
on a fall morning

in October
you goober, you
keep coming back like the Kelly
in November, I sed you

NO-VEMB-ER

Sunrise is 7:18

The seven moons I can see from this window are
streetlights on campus
The black road is white
under their light . Drops of
yesterday's rain on the fallen leaves
shine like there are spiders under those leaves, wasps and bees
as well . hide there .
They hibernate?
O bears!

On warm days, bees, wasps, hover over clots of leaves seeking entrance,
or move among the needles
on branches high in the spruce outside the
upstairs bedroom window
find, however impossibly, some way in
between the window and screen,
clenched on the sill . die there .

Winter move (ing) in
My hand creaks

I put the milk back in the icebox
They die there clenched on the sill .

Joan and the boy still sleep away upstairs
Hemlock out the window moves in the light wind
Smoke a cigarette in the dawn-dark .

97

talk to myself .
    unheard . unseen .
I look out the window at seven moons

                           (till night is gone
                            till dawn come)

           * * * * * * *

⅕ gal. Virgin Island rum, Old Boston
1 qt. straight bourbon whiskey, Mattlingly & Moore (Lawrenceburg, Indiana)
⅕ gal. tequila, product of Mexico, the Matador Distilling Co, Hartford, Conn.
               and Menlo Park, California
½ qt. left of John Begg Blue Cap scotch, fr / the Royal Lochnager Distillery,
           Balmoral (they ship it from Glasgow, Scotland, U.K.)
enuf Terry Brandy (Fernando A. de Terry, est. 1883) fr / Puerto de
           Santa Maria (coñac de Xerez)
and 2 fingers left of Pernod

          The contents of my liquor cabinet   10   days
          before you arrive. Vodka's in the refrigerator along
          with sangria and sweet vermouth de Torino. The Cali-
          fornia wines are down and cooling. Be welcome.

           * * * * * * *

Throw this one on your coordinates:

28 west out of Kingston across
the Catskill Forest Preserve to   Margaretville

30 skinnying SW along (and across) the Pepacton Reservoir, a
dammed sector of the Delaware River (eastern branch)
down past Shinhopple and Harvard, connecting with Rte. 17
                          at Eastbranch

17 west, just before Binghamton catch Interstate 81 north.

The first exit that will jolt you says McGRAW-CORTLAND.
          Don't let it tempt you; take the 2nd one, it says
              just CORTLAND . end of the ramp STOP   sign:
turn left, under the highway to the first light   (2-3
              gas stations & a Holiday Inn) : turn right
              down Clinton into town.
Two more lights will stop you at Main St. (where Clinton ends his upriver
run—but sail on, captain, my brother) right on: the street
changes name to Groton Avenue. Second light on Groton, hard
by a hamburger stand called Hardee's, steep left up the hill

98

on Graham two long blocks
                    (the college will lie on yr / right
                         dorms to your left)
                                        to
Prospect & a STOP sign.
                         Pause carefully, edge, noting especially
                         the hill coming up fr / yr / left
                         (no STOP sign there), then:
a slate-grey shingled corner house, facing Calvert (extension of Graham)
                         Cape-Cod roof;
then an awkward, more modern contrivance, aqua & white with a carport,
                         very slow:
the white-porched #60 is where we is, the driveways a foot apart. With
luck you'll see the VW wain therein, dark green, shaming the maples.
The leaves will be on the ground, brother, and the branches bare, but
         the welcome warm.

                         * * * * * * *

Alternate route: Kingston, thruway to Catskill; 23 west skimming
north end of the forest preserve, to Oneonta: left couple miles on 7,
right, back onto 23 to 26 at North Pitcher; 26 to below Cincinnatus,
41 toward McGraw and Polkville. At Polkville take 11 into Cortland.
At Main St. half-right into Tompkins, one block, I think to Prospect,
right on Prospect, around up the hill; the second intersection is the
one where you have the right of way (or that you have to look out for if
following Plan One). A churchly building on the left downhill side,
then count the three houses. Or, first white one. Where there's a will
there're two ways at least. Usually. Maybe. You take train, huh?

THESE FOOLISH THINGS

Shadow net
a net of
treebranch
shadows cover the
roof of my garage

        Sunshine, Superman, after
        a morning of heavy snow . We
        go out into the day, it's
            crisp, say, at
            $10°$ above .

Love, no paseo yet, no
promenade in old San Jan, even
the muddy or dusty streets of Boquerón escape us this year .
''Up in the air, it's a bird, it's a plane . . .''

        Sunshine on the garage roof and the net
            work, treebranch net
        a firkin of butter to cover what's left
            of the economy .

Better to think of the bills to be paid
or of getting laid three times a day . hair, clothes, life
            in disarray .
Remind me.

''He stuffed bear in a cave all winter.
Now we know.''

        The darkness wins
here . We miss those early birds, the worms
are silent as always under the slow turf . the
spruce and hemlock move their branches against the window .

     Our sense of strangeness
                    displacement
                        uneasiness   is soothed
(by the way) by the way
our bodies curl into each other . the early light
wenches thru, that freshness, then

            the busy sound of the pot flushing, the
            child waking up, cheerful for a change .
            the branches moan a bit in the cold wind.
            Day's begun.

        □

        The darkness wins
here . a car on the street outside
soon disappears, the sound of birds
            loud at dusk, subsides . We live
in this near-winter dark, live near each
other in the darkness, the boy's pre-sleep
whimper-and-moan from the next room grows also
into silence as he goes
down into sleep . We
warm one another finally . The next sound you hear
will be the radiator .

        □

What the hours are,
lines on top of the mountain in November, a
word I 'ad never noticed but in sembral terms, I
    quote an ancient allibone, an
    alley of bones now turned into
                        a
semblance . My friend Bolles stays tight with young clits, and
                        thinks he'll commit suicide by
hanging a show of his drawings on the reinforced steel
plates of a freighter headed for England,

101

see what survives a 14-day trip . An
other friend has an earache which her friend will soften by
being close enuf to be by . But the
                    question, what is the question? It is
                    another wipeshed now . The child sleeps,

Young wife, my love, climbs sleepily to the floor and sits in my lap, I ex-
plore hell, only the certainties may wed death, let all that go, I want to
K N O W when I'll be there again, when
you will .
                    zelda, granite moth, mary jane . the other
                    chances were 50% . chances
are .
                    The anchor swings like a camel-quirt these days,
                        the best stays, ma belle, not
                        mirabelle, nor kitsch, no kirsch,
what we eliminate,
not picayunes or gauloises, but
where the *N* sits at the *n* of nite, not
out of sight . profane . profound . commit, climb
into it altogether, o candle, o end of,

framboise, the eau de vie of .. How that mountaintop
looks like the plane of . the spotted trees, the lake we all saw from
                        some angle the
                        pilots differed, no matter, we
                        kept the difference ¼ even
                        we did not know the difference
            kept the anger & the love
            equal . there's a sequel? no, there
is no sequel . Read the trib tomorrow morning, there's
no sequel . wimmins lib
has take she all, Mr. Hall .
                    Donald,
                    keep your prick up . it won't last .
                        (Witches passed)
The magic stays . the boat leaves . arrives S'thhampton .
Cramped in the lifeboat, still she twitch her ass, an
equal
movement, left to right . Whatsit
                    doing?

102

that hand around my right tit?
    The hand is steady . Are you ready? Present
    passports, please.

┌──────────┐
│ *11 / 25* │
└──────────┘

                        ''Take it easy, but take it.''

Sittin by the farm house,
                    waitin for my friend to come

dog
barks in the distance
boats on the bay as well, it's
a long time, David,
we ain't had no right to some
other girl, some other time of our own, hell,
I don't know what you think of when I think of struggle, but
bit off more than he could . it was apple-blossom time in old
hat and walkin down to the farmhouse by the bay, he stood
                    for a time, listenin to dogs bark

I think of mountainsides, slickery mud between the rocks
and tree-holds under light rain, my ass full of mud in full camera.
                        mist across the eyelashes .
I think of driving 72 hours to find
they've already left . Fieldful of snow, 7 feet deep
you gotta walk thru .

                    What'll we do before lunch?
Brush the sweat off our arms, eyebrows, forehead, nose itches .
How we do not walk or climb or wait, but stand : scan ''take it
easy, but take it''
any way you can .
                            (for Tobe & David : 28.XI.70)

            □

5.XII.70 : morning conversation

I sit in the kitchen
        from the first light
                on, look at the light snow
drifted to the edge of garage roof, snuggled
                into the leaf drift

            Carlos eats

103

                  the coffee heats
                                  sky lightens to yellow
pale sunlight on
the white walls of white houses

                        He talks
                        wanting a refill on the applejuice

                        Red
                        coffeegrinder sits
                                        full of
                        new-ground coffee

                        The coffeepot coming to boil
                        talks to me .

Mint grows higher .
cigarette smokes itself in the ashtray .
Carlos lifts the cereal bowl to finish the milk

        He talks to me . His own words .

                        ☰

(the news at 5° below : for Ron & Michelle)

Wind out of the West at
      10 mph, and snow
drifts down across this hill
slowly and fine . Branches
with a ragged leaf or two   move
lightly in the wind outside the window
wisps of white blow from drifted and plowed
piles . Blue
is a color I remember
yesterday from further south . The sun
is California Dreamin' . This is the news .

Mouth pressed to another mouth
the sprit of semen, a massive unload-
ing of selves and seed . Food
for our tongues, o very nice indeed .

        Fish lie quiet beneath the frozen streams
        Ragged leaves move in the wind while
        we smile at one another in the dark .
        move near sleep .

                        104

| = = |

All that sweet, warm
blackness going down
     what do be more dream
     than real, sometime, it
     bein this grey boy talkin, after
all that hard, sweet
blackness solfening up his heart, seems I
trudge uphill thru the snowfall
thru the trees and lights and havto
spend the next two hours shovelin
sidewalk and driveway clear
of all this white shit .

| *11.XII* |

"... temperature's rising
it isn't surprising,
she certainly can ..."

The roofs are high
and the gutters deep .
      The sound of
water falling
      feeds
      our sleep . we are bound
to wrap the sky around us, while
we try to become that tree
         our bodies
      wave around
while the rain falls and the gutters run full and
the seed leaps .

| + = + = + = |

18.XII.70 : wings

Rain water this thaw, snow
water . water drops
on the needles of spruce . the wind
blows in from west southwest . Water
drips from icicles along the gutters, gutters
loosing a piss-stream of water that the wind

105

controls, wavers the stream.   The birds dream
                                    too soon of seeds.
              The top of the hemlock
cracked under the snowload last storm,
tender branches flutter and scratch the west window.
A pattern of sounds and wind .

                        What's the matter?
Driveway's clear . why worry, friend?
Words come or do not come . The thaw persists
in all our minds . A single crow far off
talks to himself .
              CAW . CAW ∕
              be well, crow .
              Find yr brothers
              someplace south of here .

6 . I . 71

We cannot agree
ever, quite, about
       the cats .
I cannot keep them by me, that close
sense, as I keep you and Carlos T., the anger
demand, needs, flow from you all, the love is
there, unequal always, never indifferent. Tangle
all this household in your mind, the kinds
of loving care we all give one another, all
       are necessary .

      And our two figures are
           set forth from Paris south,
      are set forth from Les Baux west and
      still return . Past that
      there are no more resurrections
         planned .

A week from now I put the garbage out again.
A week from now I give finals to my freshmen.
A week from now the kittens will be gone.
A week from now is payday—Joan,
you keep me sane . please

E.P. IN VENICE :   remembering April 1968, and I smile

Eagle is old man .
We sit for a bit & smoke, look
out at the snow .

Old eagle never scream anymore, he
                        keep his silence . Say
two words now and then . Go
to the restaurant next door
or the caf´ three blocks away
                        on the *canale* . sit
look out over the lagoon . Old

eagle never smoke . never talk, never
drink but maybe a half-glass of wine with meals .
Hardly touched his soup.   Remembering this,
we sit for a bit & smoke, looking out, steal
glances at bare tree shapes, shadows .

Look out at the snow.
It's near noon .
It's January .

FEBRUARY JOURNAL : 1971

Sun reaches in thru the window
strikes the kitchen wall
takes a key—click .
Clouds open and the sun hits the icebox.

      fick-fick, fick-fick,
      fick-fick, fock-fick,
      fick-fock, fick-fick, fock—

the sound of boots on snow)
         new inches overnight
         trackless white . under the black
         net of branches . yellow sun
casts a pale branchnet across the path fick-fick, fock, fick . . .

A five-minute walk in this
        barely-moving air,
my left hand inside the mitten . cold
and my left ear .
        Light gusts from the south.

        * * * * * * *

the "smoothrunning cold tides" of rain keep coming all day .
By late afternoon the temperature drops two degrees an hour
                           until
driveway cleared of slush as best can, I wonder, will I be
able to back the car out tomorrow afternoon?
how turn?
how turn her from
        an idea?
Don't mind keeping the house neat
otherwise .
Do the dishes, feed the cat, sleep
in one bed, always
sleep in one bed . otherwise the walls, other-
wise the man can separate the compost out, the
biodegradable from the dreck that
must be put out wednesdays for

the city to collect .
Build the house.
Keep it warm .

****

MARCH 1971

Snow falls and drifts
lightly beyond the window
wanders
in the light wind
        (she
        said I wrote "out-of-the-window" poems :
        it is true .)

Tape recorder and tape-deck that
fuck when so programmed, sit
erect facing me, push their
nipples out at me, try
to get me to caress their metal tits, to
flip their little switches
on . And the snow wanders out of the window . I

see there are stones on the desk, blank
tapes, cartridges, head and guide lubricant
for the double-head, the triple-head, kleenex
to wipe the whole mess up . my shirt is frayed

I have a date in Adelaide, Melbourne, Pago-Pago
14 hours from now, change
planes in San Francisco or the city of Los Angeles
for Honolulu this side of . I cross
the International Date Line solely
     to keep the date .

The wind blowth
snow fallth
branches whip in the wind
     down, rise, forth and back,
          drifts groweth summat

It's going to take us two days at least to
shovel out of this one, off to Buf-fa-lo, o
March, after all, Spring
cometh .

students walking backwards
down the hill west
against the wind . two cars
headed the other way, east across Prospect, also
crawling in reverse.

ALONG THE SAN ANDREAS FAULT

For Mark McCloskey

Low, mostly naked hills
dying scrub and rock
Juncture of Golden State and San Diego freeways
end of that american dream . Ghosts of
old insurance salesmen walk the ramps . Dairy

        Queen
        taco stands in
        valley flatlands

intersecting freeways insanely
landscaped by chickens in
constantly revolving baskets
The neon donuts blink . Other
side of the mountains / yr in the desert . Here
you really know it . Barry
Goldwater, Jr. is Congressman
These are his people .

17. IV. 71

My shoes .
I have just taken them off,
                              my shoes.
Stare out the darkened window, damn, 've
forgotten the cigarettes in the car, empty
pack in my hand, crumple it, drop it in . 2 points
Have to put my shoes back on . they
look at me reproachfully from the floor

               laces loose . their
               tongues slack.
so scruffed already they are .
& had just relaxed

Cities & towns I have to give up this year
on account of my cancer : Amster-
dam, Paris, Apt, Saignon and Aix,
(Toulouse I'll never loose), Perpignan and Dax,
Barcelona and south
                    (or the other way,
               Catania . I warn ya)
The hell, I read a review of a reading in January.
They loved me in Shippensburg, Pennsylvania.

Top of the 8th, after
four fouled off Gentry, still
2 and 2   a plastic bag
blows over home plate, Dave
Cash of the Pirates steps
     out of the box, steps
     back in, after speeding the plastic
          on its way
          with his bat, fouls
          two more off, then 3 & 2, then
infield bounce to the shortstop, out at first.

114

''Anything you want?''
     she asks, heading out the door, leading
     downstairs, get the bicycle out of the cellar .
—No, nothing, thanks. The slacks are brown, she is
carrying anything I want downstairs to take it for
a ride on the bicycle .

APRIL JOURNAL 1971
April 19 : the Southern Tier

I
look out the window in upstate New York, see
the Mediterranean stretching out below me
down the rocky hillside at Faro, three
years, two months, fourteen days earlier .
8:25 A.M.
Rosemary gone back to sleep, pink & white . I
stand at the livingroom window drinking coffee, open
the doors to the balcony . Warmth beginning, tho
I wrap my hands about the cup, count
fishing boats in the sunglare, moving shoreward now
slowly, or
sitting there motionless on the flat sea .
a fat blue arm stretches out from the coast, ripples
where the wind and currents show
muscle below the blue skin of sea
stretched out below me .
                                    The coffee's
cold toward the end of the cup . I go
back to the kitchen for more hot . put
orange in bathrobe pocket, reach for knife, return
to the balcony with the fresh cup where the flat blue sea
fills my eye in the sunglare . stretches out below me.

The Southern Tier: the maple outside the window
warms in the early sun . red buds at the ends of branches
commence their slow bursting . Green soon
                              Joan moves
          her legs against mine in the hall, goes down to
start my egg . Carlos thumps in the lower stairs . We move.

All our farewells al-
ready prepared inside us . aaaall our
deaths we carry inside us, double-yolked, the
fragile toughness of the shell . it makes
sustenance possible, makes love   possible
as the red buds break against the sunlight
possible green, as legs move against legs

possible softnesses . The soft-boiled
egg is ready now .

                         Now we eat.

When I had
finished the book
I could not remember your name, had
to turn, re
turn to the first page
to find who had written these poems .

    Fire on the mountain, light
    crossing a bridge between
    the twin peaks of death and
        the blind eye
    of God, your father . Burt,
never
the boat on the sea, never
the horse in the mountain .
  Blood in the dirt, Burt, Federico
  is dead,
& no one knew who he was .
    el barco sobre el mar
    y el caballo en la montaña.
y una aguja de luz en el centro
de tu cabeza, hombre .

Between   5   sonnets by Bill Bronk
and   6   poems by Carl Rakosi,
    I take   3   or   4   sips of my milkshake (coffee)
    from the Friendly Ice Cream Corp.
    from a straw
                    Wilbraham, Mass.,
and my son wakes up from his nap, comes
to climb in my lap.
kicks the book from the table
onto the floor . what more
can I say? It's one
           way to begin a long summer.   haha.

31 . V . 71

JOURNAL 31 . V . 71   late weather
Crabapple blossoms white,
              tight to the branches, dwarf
trees in front of the building . mid-quad . Mist
in the morning
sun in the afternoon
million flowers .
              May 31st, & the evening weather report
     showed a sparkling of
snow into the Sierras on
the California side, Lake Tahoe . O

              blossoms here
              in Cortland now, the
              tulips near gone by, but
              Nevada City
              caught it . snow!
Gary got it this time.

WHAT'S UNTIED ON WHITSUNTIDE?

The last nite before June, I lean
     over the hot air register
     to warm my hands .
     Ate ⅛ of a banana
     threw it up.
     I count the Pentecost
                    I throw it up.
                    I plan.

MARY LAIRD
is not afeard
Walter Hamady
keeps her happy
morning, afternoon, and

''Always merry and bright'' is
not a girlscout motto, Mary,
                right?

                Rain   again-
                st the
                windows

drums
down
on the roof,
hard in Walter's
garden
                the syndrome is
                / was /   talk

Were met
watering can in one hand   (we had
interrupted that work upon the garden
at 6 P.M.—what proved
unnecessary finally)   so—

The talk was helpful, tho,
as was the eating & drinking
                Ed brought the roast & rice
                and talked
                tenderly to my wife about carpets
                one eye warming to the task
                of making two new eyes see
                the colors, the pattern, the wear
that hung that rug on the kitchen wall :
the care of the owners to place it there

121

(light from the kitchen windows
colors move .

But now past midnite :   rain on the roof
thunder in the air   lightning in the sky
the cat throwing up in the kitchen .
Everyone else asleep but me &
          the barfing cat
               Lightning scatters the trees
they run
about the sides of this valley between flashes
the cat comes to my left foot, stands, paws on my knees & purrs
               crosseyed & clean . I mean
          rain on the roof, they call it
patter? Lightning leaps across
We wonder at the thunder, the
cat and I . Cows
on the hillside, huddle under the storm . Caught out
they / we
          are all asleep & warm
          The talk helped . the rain
               comes . the trees dance.

ALL US FLOWERS
                    (living for the moment)

LIKE IT LOTS.

                    I drank some wine tonite .

                    ''Schools closed when they drove the cattle
                    past—a thousand head lowing and bellowing
                    . . . Cattle after cattle went by until at last a
                    wagon with an old bearded man, sober-faced
                    and silent. He is too rich and full of thought
                    to have a good time like the others.''

                    Lehtinen's *History of Jaffrey, New
                    Hampshire*

Goodby old cattle baron, goodby
old baron and drovers . We
shall not look upon your like again, goodby
old sweethearts and pals . I want you two

122

                    to have these two
              pieces of stone . Keep
              them as yr / own
to remember this moment.

Try it on, try it on   .   We have a future in carpets .

                  PD county truck
              La maize pousse
          et les choufleurs
The former, he
kneel behind his cultivator
joust the motor .   Irregular patches
                           looking like islands
                           of old snow, dot
                           the upper meadows
lie along the ridges to the west . oho, the glacier
driving thereover .

Carl is not coming to the reading . he has papers to correct
Marcia is not coming to the reading . she has a new baby
Joan is not coming to the reading . Carlos T. wants to
        play with the new baby & won't sleep
Walter is not coming to the reading because he thinks Carl will be there
        besides, Diane arrived today for a visit, and she
        was at the reading in Milwaukee yesterday
Gerth is not coming to the reading because he's behind time as usual
        and thinks that 9 o'clock is too late .
It's my reading . I take Marcia's mother to the reading .
A pleasant surprise, Mary and Ed are at the reading .
I forgot to get batteries for my cassette recorder today
        no one else records it .
I read until 10:30 . It's a good reading.

THE FARM

Goats in the oats
stoats are in the shoats

the karma's in the barn

the house is in the valley
        past the bridge
                (narrow bridge)

bitchin' in the kitchen
drinkin' coffee & cognac
at 4 in the morning

The girl is in the bed
        with her own head

The poet's downstairs
        with his two ears
                & cold hands . We

do what we can . This
cognac isn't bad .
It's Martell .

                        The moon is down, the
                        light'll be up soon

                        o hell,
                        The sin is in the not doing.
                        The farmer's in the dell.

                        Nothing is well.

LA LISIÈRE

How we move
about the wealth
of friendships :
too often at the edge of it

How rare, the move to center
        where we live

Selvage, that word,
each of us stands shyly

at the edge of woods

fearing the valley
chary of the sun
waiting .

Carl's eyes at parting, turning away, not
wanting to let go   . We

all go the way we go
all the way . we
go, each his own
way . we all go
away . we go.

The tide runs high, the
evening star explodes .

What   is the sign
we mean to live by, we
mean, to live by . (?)

---

seething anger
silent cunt . cat
got her tongue . she
is very young.

It's 3:15 in the Midwest now
Time for poets to be in bed
       not up and scribbling.
       I'm down .
       The coffee heats
       I'm downstairs
       I'm shot down . shit up
Shut up & keep dreaming
drink the coffee
drink the cognac
We all sleep sometimes, we
all come back

sometimes .

                                        1st   we win
                                        2nd   is place
                                        3rd we show

                    1st Person,
                    very singular
                    First is place
                    where . what
                    we show is secondary

            First we show
            Second we win (or lose)
            Third is place
                        (second
                        person

Cooze we lose
when we show, win
or place
            (is person .

Which is, if we win,
what we win

Place IS person
                    where
if we are lucky
we can show where,
     win or place .

D R A W !
                    (smile,
            when you say that, friend.)

All three women are
Stacked .
                    So are the cards.
                          W H A C K !

126

LIKENON

Like
in
    on the stone

Lie, kin
        on the stone

Lichen on the stone

---

envoi in mid-June ╱ WALTER GOES TO THE GARDEN & GETS A HARDON

> "Ate a whole row of radishes .
> They were crisp."
> —Mary Hamady

Your teeth & Walter's
crunching down into
those bowlsful of radishes
        red & white & firm
rhymes with lettuce . swiss chard . spinach .
green onions . yum.

                    Mary, please,
        forget the nightshade soup &
        the jimsonweed salad, huh?

                17 . VI . 71

TRANSLATION

(replies to a New York Quarterly questionnaire)

1. In your view, what is a translator?

A man who brings it *all* back home.
In short, a madman.

2. What special qualifications must a translator have?

He must be willing (& able) to let another man's life enter his own deeply enough to become some permanent part of his original author. He should be patient, persistent, slightly schizoid, a hard critic, a brilliant editor, and have an independent income . . .

3. Is there any rule regarding the choice of subject matter for a translator? Should the translator stay away from any given original? Is it important that the translator be temperamentally close to the original, or the author of the original?

Stay away from third-rate work and outright shit. There's nothing to be gained but money and not much of that. If you don't love what you read in the original, or admire some major part of it, forget it. We are all hundreds, maybe thousands of people, potentially or in fact. Affinities help. Theoretically possible for a man who hates himself, say, to make a fine translation of someone whose work he *hates*. Do not think I have ever seen such a translation. Incompetence or beaky egotism are something else.

4. Should a translator ever "improve" on the original? If so, under what circumstances?

First of all, it's hardly ever possible. One is lucky to be able to make an equivalent value. Most "improvements" prove to be distortions of one variety or another. If the distortion permits a more perfect Englished version consistent with the diction and style of the translation, then perhaps, yes. Here we get into matters of taste. Geniuses ought not to translate, unless they be truly mad.

5. To what extent may a translator introduce variations which his own language permits, but the original language does not?

To a reasonable extent, if the distortion of meaning be not too great. Equivalencies are different in different tongues and different generations. Who's expected to read the final job?

6. How far should a translator attempt to "modernize" an antiquarian piece?

Try first to find a diction, a modern diction which will translate as many values as possible of the original. I've seen Latin poetry translated into hip language that works very well for given pieces. Carried too far, of course, over a whole body of work, it'd be a stunt. Some stunts, however, are brilliantly executed. It evens out.

7. What is the best way for a translator to approach the problem of multiple associations of word choice? Multiple meanings? (polysemia)

If the double-meaning or an equivalent is impossible in English, he chooses whichever single meaning seems most genial to his English text, or strongest to his understanding. Overtones are constantly being lost. Let him approach polysemia crosseyed, coin in hand.

8. Must unit and line length be preserved under all circumstances?

No. You're talking about poetry here. If the original is interesting for its meaning, translate the meaning. If the meaning is irrelevant by comparison with the musical values of the piece, translate, as best possible, what Pound calls "the *cantabile* values." But choose, so you know WHAT it is you're doing.

9. What is the difference between free and strict, literal translation? between free translation and outright adaptation?

Very often readability. Strict translation usually makes for stiff English, or forced and un-english rhythms. Outright adaptation is perfectly valid if it makes a good, modern poem. Occasionally, an adaptation will translate the spirit of the original to better use than any other method: at other times, it will falsify the original beyond measure. Much depends upon the translator (also upon the reader).

10. What frauds have been foisted on the public recently? (And not so recently?)

Yo no sé.

11. Do you experience psychological impediments in translation? (Blocks, slips, unconscious mistakes?)

Starting a project is always difficult; it means rearranging one's whole time to make some continuity (of time and thought) fit. Done slowly enuf, moving into the author's head should present no problems, if one is ready for it. The process might make a few problems in one's life, however. That's part of the dues.

12. Why do you translate at all? How does it relate to your work? What long and short range effects does it have? What defects?

Complicated. I'm interested in the original for whatever reason. I'm

interested in the language and the processes of language. Pace and time. Take that earlier answer: *yo no sé*. It's different in pace and overtone from *no se* or I dunno, or *weiss nicht*, or *sais rien*, or *non so*. Next question: usually my work will relate to it. It fills time when my own head is not working at poems regularly. There's an interaction. The long range effect is some kind of enrichment of human understanding. Short range? Everything from giggles to rage to a sense of words whose weight and meaning have changed, are changing. The sea of language. Defects? Sometimes I can no longer think English. Not sure that's a defect, tho it must be remedied before the job is delivered. Alternately: it gives me something else to do, so I don't have to write poems. But that's true also of my 17-month-old son who has a half-translatable language of his own, but IS no language, nor work of artlessness . . . .
Suppose I liked horses better, or fencing, or were entomophogous?

13. At the end of his interview in NYQ issue #2, Paul Blackburn commented:

I do enjoy translating, getting into other people's heads.

Thass right . . .

This is one motivation for translation. Are there others?

There must be . . .

Thank you for your time.

Quite all right. Thank you.

Marina Roscher
for NYQ

Sitting in the tub
waiting for the ache in
my shoulders to go away

.

                    nerves shlow down, the
                    muscles relax .

The tax is refunded in full . I feel
the skinnyness of arms, the bony chest
cavity, front & back, as I soap up .

It's something else for the fingertips to remember
I haven't had a body like this since I was   15 .
What is it the ribs remember, the clavicles, the
        wingbones so unfleshed?
        To recognize the differences
in the quality of flesh tho, something else .

                [+   +]

a doomed man planting tomatoes
backyard of a house he lives in
belongs to somebody else . kneeling
on the earth
his hands move earth
feeling earth .

                [+   +]

T H E   2   A.M.
of a summer night in Cortland, this street
            high on the hill is
virtually (virtuously?) soundless, it
            has the virtue of near
            silence   .   The far
sound of a truck, mile away on the interstate,
a bird or two waking up (hence thee, fear), two
faucets that run (do not drip to the nearest), the
            sound of my fat pen
            writing this down .

The bath room faucets sound like the overrun
            of a fountain in Granada .
            The birds go back to sleep.
The truck climbs away north toward Homer, Preble,
Tully, Syracuse . just the sound of fountain, no breeze.

How say goodnite to you all, dear friends?
Easy.
Goodnite!   The bed
awaits my head,
waits on the
sound of this pen
stopping now .

                                    12 . VI . 71

JOURNAL: JUNE 1971

The spruce outside the bedroom
        window is full of wasps and
                bees again this year . The
birdfeeder's nailed further down the other side the tree
        high enuf for birds, low enuf for me to fill it
                from the ground . Yesterday,
Joan saw two cardinals close up . A pair
: bright red of the male, reddish buff of the
        lady . stayed around calling all
                morning . made her day .

13 . VI . 71

Picked up the wire fencing today at the lumberyard
150 feet of it (having paced out the back) and
14   stakes, got
it home & realized I had no maul to
drive them with   . . . nor the strength nor weight
these days . To make an oversized
playpen of the backyard
anyway puts my head in the tree .
Where are the bees? The yard dies, the
tulips go by, what fun!
I write letters these days to everyone .

14 . VI . 71

SAILBOAT

reflected in the lake .. The
rectangles of iron, so
composed, the waves are so
      hang there rusting
      lightly at the seams . below
      the door to the garden opens
      on a field . there
            is the green in evidence,
            the tree . hello!
            these many years back,
            Robert Creeley!

15.VI.71

How it turns
in again, the pain
    across my shoulders these mornings .

       Possession of the mind
       a fragile thing / when the pain
       goes,
then's the time to use it . what's left of it .

    ☐

Men with shovels directed a stream
of sizable pebbles into the excavations
about young new-planted mountain ash trees
set mid-quad in the concrete
from a dump truck .
I brought back home
a single rhododendron bloom that had fallen .

    ☐

    Greg & I had measured and sunk
9 of the stakes and had started stretching the wire.
There was not enuf muscle between us to stretch the first length tight
(Greg is a strong young man) . We quit . call in reinforcements .

Outside the cellar door, I spoke to a bee, he
danced before me, crotch to face, he checked me out, he
      buzzed, I talked, he sat
        in my beard for a moment . We
          talked. I wanted to go inside . I told him
            so . I did . The phonecalls
               worked.

Howard & Al & Jerry arrived about 5
We all got drunk, did half the work (the first
    hundred feet are the hardest?)

      Then had supper .

             16.VI.71

12:30 A.M.
June 17th

Way over to work tonite
I followed the walks assiduously, feet
    clicking the concrete
    dried from the morning's rain.

After writing poems for an hour or some
thing like that, the way back I angled across
lawns
    walks
        gravel
            never
                mind the ache in the shoulder, in the
right leg, so it's damp, it's
the shortest way home .

        □

9:20 A.M.

      C O R N
8 in. to a foot high in some fields

Flocks of blackbirds cross the roads and land . talk .

    black . talk . back

The cows are merely silent and further away. Queer.
One red-winged blackbird, his orange trim,
crosses the windshield, flirts his tail . Good

M O R N I N G, dear
               milkmen!

        □

9:45

Allison likes the music boxes
Allison likes the pink telephone
and the white telephone .
               Carlos T.
   develops a sense of property .

Livingroom loud with both their angry tears

        □

10:05
Robins on the lawn

always facing away . attentive.

☐

12:30 S U N S H I N E   S U P E R M A N

I.   Buttercups .
gardeners & tools along the walks.
            another robin, Donovan.

II.   Walking the power mower along
         the slope   single-handed .
               phys-ed major .

            ☐

TOP floor, then
when I look out, I look
out into the tree
outside .

        (This is not a
        plea for the economy)
            but

It's nice to think
(Carlos running & laughing downstairs
    Joan joking with him)

there is nothing we need .

"KITTY KAT!   PAPPI!"
      my son suggests,
      pounding at my door,
      lightly, tho .
"Where's your truck?"
                 It
is not an alternative.

And the cat's in the
     laundryroom   having supper.

                             17 / VI / 71

JOURNAL: JUNE 1971

Three hawks over the northern Catskills
North Pitcher, Norwich, past Oneonta
    23 across the state .
Honey at Hunter on 23A .
across the river, the Kelly,
    nearly awake, smiles .

18.VI.71

It's   2   minutes before midnite . I
am about to read   2   poems, no
3   poems of Bobby Byrd's
see where the magic comes in.
It does.
It is human and inhuman

    It are the birds on the dump.
    They fight . the feathers
    fall. The feathers are
    dark & bright .
        That's all.

20.VI.71

S H A D O W of a large bird
                              floats
down the sunny half of the road
              runs west to east   .   We

here, under the shade of trees, south
                    side of the street
wait for the lizard to come,
for the cat to arrive at the roof window
                        calling for entrance .

We are hungry animals prowling this road.

I wonder, I S   I T   A L L   L O V E ?

We lie here in the shadow of the afternoon
          shadow of the bedclothes   slipped up .

Love & hunger   .   the bird

        the lizard, the cat,

                ourselves   .   Treecrown shadows

move over this half of the street, over
driveway and gutter.   down.
                                leaf shadow.

                        22 . VI . 71

redefinitions

Take off another man's style
in a poem about flying . takeoff of the plane .
Mid-flight, the hostesses
take off their clothes & sit in the passengers' laps .
    Call the poem: TAKEOFF.

                        22.VI.71

ALPHABET SONG

Before men
were gods, animals
were themselves, no
sense of immortality we
can speak of.   How
            live with one another
            somehow, never
            was no problem . The

god wears a jackal's head, the
lion the head of a woman, the
gorgons were the man's protectors on
                a long journey . We
carry the W O R D   with us.
Come now, read: there's
            a new world comin'

25 . VI . 71

"TO THE REAR, HARCH!—to the
       right front, harch!"
                              (hup, 2—)
The blossoms
in the jar, the
petals on the roses are
beginning to fall to the table . The
wild flowers have sense enuf to close up tight
                                   for the night .
       "GET THAT FORMATION TIGHT, CLOSE IT UP!"
We do .

The girls spread out on the sand
            in the sun, half-
thinking, half-
listening to the remarks, half
               asleep . Why move at all?
                         The sun.
keeps us talking
            L O V E   &   D E A T H
            P L A N T S   N O W   R E A D Y
    Petunias, pansies, snaps, alyssum, early cabbage,
    sweet spanish onions, LARGE selection of geraniums,
    all colors, and perennials. Urns filled . . .

Urns filled with specifically precious, precious

What is it, Tim, we can fulfill
       after specifically precious Death, we
       speak to.   Will I talk to you then, fill
       yr / ears with words . I want to

    [Do not want that.   Let
       each man's words be his own.]

                                        It

                    smiles at me
from underneath the table . That
green and yellow
ball .

Or what severances are offered?
what the doctors predict, what
the gods prescribe?

                              How can we
offer it all, Paul? how
ignore the earth movers . will
take it all down?

You ask a lot of questions tonite. Enuf of that .
                                       The cats

move quietly about the house, lie
down where it is most comfortable
to lie . As
the goat bucks his leash, it snaps
tight, the
two-year length of that rope, tonite, love,
so buck I .

Figure that last year.   I want
to set it . year-after-next
                   hopefully without pain

          N O T H I N G   I   C A N ' T   S T A N D !

               I don't believe that either .
Let
the mountain be set
the house there forever
a final summer
gazing at the sun.
        Mediterranean .

27. VI. 71

sundaysundaysundaysundaysunday
sun
day
a quiet along the empty walks
single bird speaks to blue sky to
elm heavywith summer
E M P T Y A N D A L I V E
E M P T Y A N D A L I V E
E M P T Y A N D A L I V E
The simple act of drinking a cup of coffee
The simple act of pulling up one's trousers
buckling the belt . having shit, washed hands and face,
go to work . empty and alive . heavy with summer . light
with the promise of death . bright books in the bookcase,
window open, the day comes in, o fade the carcinoma, lay
down the two dollars, all those others rolling dice, but
it's my body, I'll bet on that . o, it floats thru the blood
with the greatest of ease . the pain goes and comes again . the
cat hunts in the grass, the gull swings over the sea, the blood
sings a very old tune . Take it
easy, it's sunday, no?
All day.

If the chairs are comfortable, why
    not sit in them?

I hunch on the top rail of a fence in
    the sun . whitewashed.

Six ducklings squeak, follow one an-
        other, a straggling line down
        past the adjacent building into the weeds .

They're panicked by trucks oiling &
graveling & rolling out
the yard of this garage. Andre
with folded arms, impassively
twitches his moustache in the doorway, checks
the line of gravel-dump.

One duckling's gotten trapped
in the growth of weeds alongside the building hiding.
        I free it.

Another's got covered with burdocks : overweight,
it falls on its back & can't get up . I
clear enough burrs off its head and neck
so it can rise : it runs. Tough. It's
bound to get caught again.
Where's the mother?

Two bulbs replaced in the back, and
the left tail lens the mechanic broke by stepping on it.
The Gaucelm Faidit Uzerchemobile has been in-
spected, the State of New York, 1972 .

30 . VI . 71

THE PARTICI-
        (pants are abt to descend)
pants are about to descend
July the 5th, this
Year of Our Nixon, 1971, upon
       Tom Jefferson
(within the infrastructure of
Grand Valley (Mich.) State College)
      for a festival of poesy!
Goodbye, minions of Dave Lorenz!
Hello, poets!

        PB
        Unofficial Greeter

reductio ad suburbium

Plymouth (Mass.)
variety of mailboxes,
   Glad ys avenue, Grand
     Haven (Mich.), bearing
a likely number
       (1640)

—You can
see the backs of their Bermuda shorts
when they turn on the lawn sprinklers,
                   Susan says .

                        5. VII. 71

JOURNALS: JULY 1971

July 15

Over the river soundlessly
a fish jumps . Late sun
along the Maumee—or the Sandusky—
assuming it's the Sandusky River flows thru
Sandusky into Lake Erie at that point—
at 8 A.M., Cool morning, two
ducks, a pair, no, a brace of ducks,
wing it, their long necks stretched up
over the river soundlessly.
(A fish jumps).

Interstate 81 North . late sun, 8:30 P.M., on the
Pennsylvania hills .
Crossing state line, the rest area
has but one vehicle in it. I
miss the Uzerchemobile!

Big lovely clouds to the north after sundown .
Great purple fish pursued by great violet dog
in a pink sea . Mediterra-nean. San
dusky is far, o far.
Last light in the sky
drops spatter the windshield
Thunderstorm greets us home .

July 17

Lines of sunlight across the base of the skull
    Windows shining . Trees move .
        Mysterious skull bumps.
        Roll tenderly against the wood.

149

July 18

Barn smell, old wood, hayloft .
Out over the cut fields, a fat
goldfinch, black-&-yellow
    moves heavily .

                only larks flit.

July 23

Hermes
in dark glasses
Mercury in shades

at the cafeteria table with
three other shades (Tom, Al, Sonia)
    sits, dis-
cussin the news
from De-troit, Californ-ya,
    many other fine places .

Wednesday lunch: I think it was Armand
came worriedly over, asked me:
    "Is David here?"   (David's day
                     to read with me
                     and Gregory &
                     Donald Hall)
"Right over that table there.'

From a far country,
David Henderson has
come unto Michigan,
Hermes in shades, to
    give us the word, BURN.

               (signed) Paul Blackburn

20 . VII . 71

Branches bend
in the wind, leaves
wave thru the window at me,
          and whistle .

I'm very popular today.

Gloria, Carlos T., and Joan
are down at Steve and Nancy's

Male cat comes in thru the window
      to talk to me. The
room is filled with evening light
3 hours yet to sundown. Hey!
          it's summer!

---

evening fantasy :

Traveling ahead again
in my head again
which cannot know that I'm dead again .
Beshit, fathered, and Magillicuddy
        am I?

People to talk with in those streets
        delight me
Spicer, I am not afraid :
Olson as a gigantic cherub
      garbed in nightgown, thinking;
Steve Jonas rolling happily for once in angeldust;
Kerouac writing the true novel of the Golden Eternity
on a ribbonless typewriter, without paper, never revising

Some time   finally to talk with Dr. Williams,
tho it seems I stammer,
he don't

              ''if you like it, we
              like it too,
              we clued it with you''

151

and I, beyond all likelihood, get to that grove before Ezra,
walk about, saying:
"I must prepare, I must
prepare."

22.VII.71

Young, dying yellow birch on Owego St.
    half-block from the IGA .

fat black ants tool along beside me
or troll across the sidewalks . I am careful

Because I think maybe words are coming, I sit
on a stump in the sun in front of number 28,
staring at pink and white hollyhocks under its front windows,
an ambivalent paleness of hollyhock .
I always thought they were a
            somewhat gross plant,
                those scratchy leaves .

The running samaritan this noon-hour, I've
delivered a bottle of freshmade orange juice iced, &
a suppository   25 mg. Adult .
insert one as directed for vomiting . and am
on my way
to the IGA
for cigs and a cold 6-pak of Coca Cola for Howard
to help celebrate
his first post-celebration-of-being-21 day .

Beware friends and well-meaning bar owners bearing gifts
that resemble three fingers high of excellent bourbon in a whiskey sour glass,
beware even the double shot . uh, *stark!*

On the way back to Tomkins St,
the ants accompany me in the hot sun. Don't
they know that sidewalks are terrible places to cruise,
for ants anyway?

And we always treated hollyhocks like
second class citizens, poor relations, bums, we
kept them out by the garage in back.

Those delicate blooms.
The awkward stems.
The hairy leaves.

23 . VII . 71

"Sorry to keep you waiting, sir—"
        —That's all right
            All the time in the world—
                (pleased voice of the operator)
                    "Thank you!"

That hour of night . It
must be so for all of us .

23 . VII . 71

Mist rising along the ridges of hills
mist rising from the surfaces of ponds
        Homer, Preble, Dante's
hell or English countryside . Fast, we
go over hills & roads, across
the city of Syracuse to the airplane
takes us West .

            ====

We manage the flight to Chicago okay
—Joan's flying student standby—even
manage to sit together, with a member of
the Board of Trustees for Roberts Wesleyan
sitting window seat, who,
taking Joanie for student, asks about
student / professor relationships.
        Some nerve, I'd say. At
O'Hare I find out Paul Carroll's middle
initial, that he now lives on North Mohawk,
is D., and from Inara that his office number
University of Illinois, is 633-2285.

        Then disaster:
only the military standbys make it on.
I wave out window sadly, in case she's there behind
        the rain-stained glass. I'm in, she's out
or: She's in, I'm out here, but *we're* not
        out of O'Hare . We seem
to be twelfth in line for takeoff, & taxi
        a lot, slowly . The captain

153

even turns off the NO SMOKING sign
I have a cigarette . I have a second.
20 minutes after departure time
Joan and I are both on the ground, still,
except we're turning a corner toward another runway
& Joan is checking out the next two sets of possibilities
we know the direct at 3:55 arrives Boise at 6:20.

+ + + +

10:36 the sign goes on, I don't get to
finish the 2nd cigarette, and
at 10:36½ we're air
borne, bound in separate
elements, bound by seatbelt in air
or grounded in snackbar, o we've
been there before. I think
I'll drink, and read, then sleep.
Try to ripoff the airlines, will we? They'll show us.
Five minutes before 11, we cross the Mississippi.

* * * * *

Iowa, Nebraska, small white clouds far below (we're
some 26,000 ft. Then over
Rock Spring, Wyoming, the Continental Divide
coming up. Groundspeed
520 mph

What a gas, maybe
Louie Armstrong & I
die, back to back,
cheek to cheek, maybe the same year. "O,
I CAN'T GIVE YOU
ANYTHING BUT LOVE,
Bay-aybee"
1926, Okeh a label then
black with gold print, was
one of my folks' favorite tunes, that year
that I was born . It is all still true
& Louie's gone down &
I, o momma, goin down that same road.
Damn fast.

154

+ + + +

Salt Lake City's hot .
      cragged & scorched, the mountains
            to the east .
The desert begins, the
desert's hard . I buy
4 postcards of the desert
(after checking for Joan's alternates
      with a desk clerk at United
I climb back on the plane slowly, this heat. She may
         arrive Boise
         4:50 or
         6:20)

Salt flats and brackish water
as I take off
in the heat.

+ + + +

Take a shit at 5:15
A.M., Cortland, N.Y.

Fly about 2,000 miles and in
Boise, Idaho, some
literal 12 hrs., 35 minutes later,
      take another shit.

Bigod, I must have been full of shit.

+ + + + +

July 28, 1971

155

Photo: Caryl Eshleman

PAUL BLACKBURN was born on November 24, 1926, in St. Albans, Vermont. He spent his youth in Vermont, New Hampshire, South Carolina, and New York City. He attended NYU and the University of Wisconsin (from which he received his BA in 1950). He received a Fulbright Grant in 1954 and spent two years at the University of Toulouse in southern France and then lived in Spain until 1957 when he returned to New York City. He made a living as an editor and a translator until 1967 when a Guggenheim Fellowship took him back to Europe, where many of these *Journals* were written. In 1969 he moved to Cortland and taught at the State University there.

Blackburn was a splendid translator of El Mio Cid, Cortazar, Paz, Picasso and the entire canon of Provençal lyric poetry.

He died on September 13, 1971, in Cortland, New York.